The Art of Leadership

A Choreography of Human Understanding

Zach Kelehear

ROWMAN & LITTLEFIELD EDUCATION
Lanham, Maryland • Toronto • Oxford
2006

Published in the United States of America
by Rowman & Littlefield Education
A Division of Rowman & Littlefield Publishers, Inc.
A wholly owned subsidiary of The Rowman & Littlefield Publishing Group, Inc.
4501 Forbes Boulevard, Suite 200, Lanham, Maryland 20706
www.rowmaneducation.com

PO Box 317
Oxford
OX2 9RU, UK

British Library Cataloguing in Publication Information Available

Library of Congress Cataloging-in-Publication Data

Kelehear, Zach.
  The art of leadership : a choreography of human understanding / Zach Kelehear.
     p. cm.
  Includes bibliographical references and index.
  ISBN 1-57886-238-8 (pbk. : alk. paper)
  1. Educational leadership. 2. School supervision. 3. Design. I. Title.
LB2806.K42 2005
371.2—dc22

                                                         2005002418

∞™ The paper used in this publication meets the minimum requirements of
American National Standard for Information Sciences—Permanence of
Paper for Printed Library Materials, ANSI/NISO Z39.48-1992.
Manufactured in the United States of America.

To my children, Hannah and Ben
and
To my love and my magic light, Karen

Contents

Acknowledgments

I owe thanks to many people for helping me accomplish this work. First, I thank Dr. Karen Heid, my wife, for being my soul mate and for bringing me to a whole new level of appreciation for life and for art. She listened patiently, prodded often, and supported always. This work would not have been possible without her. Secondly, I thank my children, Hannah and Ben, for being patient with my writing and for helping me see life with the wonder and excitement that only children can imagine. For them, living each day is itself an act of art making. I thank my parents, Kal and Kathryn Kelehear, for supporting me even when it was not clear where I was headed. They have always found a way to love me in spite of myself. And to my brother, Sparky Kelehear, I offer my appreciation. All children should be so lucky as to have a brother as kind and supportive as you.

I am indebted to Richard Siegesmund for his invaluable insight into the world of art and aesthetics and for his powerful editing, which helped my writing say what I meant for it to say. He has been gentle but firm in helping me see the holes in my thinking, and throughout he has remained a good friend. I also thank Joseph Norman for his valuable contribution of artwork. His work helps make my message so much clearer than I could manage through text alone. And I thank Ed Pajak, a leader in the world of supervision, who has become a mentor to me as I continue to struggle with so many confounding and important questions. Finally, I remain grateful to Ray Bruce for his unending support of my journey even when it seemed I had lost my way.

A word about the artwork of Joseph Norman. Throughout this work I have used Joseph Norman's images from his *Amazing Grace* portfolio project. As chair of the Art Department at the University of Georgia's Lamar Dodd School of Visual Art, Joe has come to understand leadership in exciting, if sometimes painful, ways. He reminds me often, over coffee in downtown Athens, Georgia, that his experiences as printmaker and painter, as an art educator, as a college athlete, and as a child of the projects have all prepared him to understand the powerful role of leaders in creating positive places for our children. His art included in this book serves in part to confront the viewer with what a colleague of his calls the "complex, tangled, and daunting" (Taylor, p. 11) realities of today's living. Joe's works are indeed complex, tangled, and daunting, and I have certainly come to appreciate the parallels to leading in today's schools.

I have placed an example of each of the "Elements of Art" and the "Principles of Design" beside the "Artist's View." I have not selected necessarily the best choices, but I have made decisions that made sense to me. So, if I have erred or mishandled Joe's work, the responsibility is entirely mine. But I thank Joseph Norman for the courage to allow me to pick and choose from his collection and in so doing allow me a chance to engage his work as I have tried to engage my view of leadership and supervision. Leadership is indeed a complex, tangled, and daunting undertaking.

Foreword

Years ago, when I taught advanced placement world history in high school, I had the pleasure, and the challenge, of working with some of the school's finest and brightest students. Almost without exception, the students who created some of the more perplexing challenges were the artists. They were as bright as other students, but their approach to my linear and simple teaching of Western civilization challenged me to revisit many of my assumptions about teaching and learning. Simply put, they saw things differently, and they encouraged me to do the same. I was never quite sure what went on at the other end of the building, where the art room (and band room, chorus room, shops, and special education classes) was positioned. I was pretty certain, however, that its geographic position suggested that the art teacher and her students lived in another world.

Fortunately for me, and ultimately my students, the art teacher and a student we shared took me on as a special "project" and helped me stretch beyond thinking of artists as magicians, although in many ways this is what they are. The student worked with me for a week during the lunch period, in the lobby where all students and staff could watch, on perspective and the use of "vanishing point." She struggled to help me understand. She used the language of art, and through the experience I began to understand the process of making art. Equally important, I trusted her to guide and support me. I trusted her to lead me, and she trusted me to take risks and to be vulnerable. What the art teacher and her student taught me was more than technique and skill. They revealed to me that through the medium of their art they were having conversations about things that really mattered, just as I had tried to do in my history classes, but were doing so in a different language. Theirs was the language of art. And that language was based in part on an understanding of the elements of art and principles of design.

At the core of the student's and my work was the relationship that emerged from the shared experience. The process was fun, and the product turned out nicely. But it was the relationship that lasted and that mattered. I have come to believe that relationships are at the center of all meaningful endeavors. Take, for example, artists who are successful in large part because they were able to develop relationships with their subjects. The artists saw it, felt it, sensed it, and understood it. In a similar way, viewers of art often "connect" with a particular work, and in so doing they begin to develop a relationship with the object of their observation. This visceral sense of relationship is core to Dewey's (1934) sense of aesthetics.

In like fashion I recognize that the art of successful living is a function of healthy relationships. If we talk about good families, we often describe ones where trust, understanding, and communication are evident in daily living. When we study successful teachers, we frequently discover that the teacher and students have cultivated a relationship of mutual understanding and shared experiences. In this same vein, Lewis (2004) notes that "student success depends on three qualities of teaching: content knowledge, pedagogy, and strong relationships with students" (p. 483). Out of the last note, that of relationship, we again recognize that when there exists a significant and meaningful connection between students and teachers, students do well because they feel safe, noticed, and supported. And upon examination of successful school leaders, we find that trust and communication are the sine qua non of authentic leaders.

Teachers trust the instructional leadership. Teachers feel safe, noticed, and supported. Certainly there are many successful managers of programs in today's schools, but the most effective leaders recognize the role of relationships. Drawing on Howard's discussion of the craft of artists, Blumberg (1989) notes that a successful supervisor is one who understands the craft of developing a "nose" for what is going on in the school. By being "in" the schools with teachers, by not being "of" the teachers, school leaders can develop relationships that strike the important, albeit difficult, balance between closeness and distance. For school leadership, both are required. A successful principal knows the teachers by being in the school and by knowing the various and simultaneous instructional enterprises in the school. "Without a highly developed nose, an administrator has no basis for understanding what is happening around him or her," (p. 56) and teachers are far less likely to respond to the leader's comments when they sense a lack of relevance between the principal's world and theirs.

Understanding and cultivating relationships may come in various forms: from principal to teacher, teacher to student, or community to school. It may also come in the form of pedagogy to curriculum, core values to daily practice, or superintendent to board of education. Whichever form it might come in, successful schooling is a function of relationships. When the relationship between school leadership and teaching staff loses authenticity, the students are lost in the "disconnect" between teacher and leader.

We in leadership positions have a special obligation and responsibility to understand our own and other's humanity. The most immediate way that we begin to strike this understanding is when we take time to listen, both to ourselves and to others. Covey (1989) speaks to this fundamental recognition when he demands that successful leaders seek first to understand, then to be understood. But listening in relationships is only part of the challenge. Equally important, leadership in schools also necessitates the capacity for relational thinking. It is in this context that I have come to the belief that leadership in general and supervision in particular are best understood when they are viewed as an art form. The language of art, the craft of art making, and the aesthetic of art evaluation bring to the school leader a mechanism for relational thinking.

Very quickly, as one becomes familiar with the language of art discussion and evaluation, he or she can begin noting that value and meaning of a given piece are entirely specific to a situation, setting, or circumstance. Just as many different artists display their work in a museum, the evaluation of that work for the viewer becomes a function of the relationship between various elements and principles that may or may not be present in the work. Similarly, I suggest in this writing that leadership is best described, analyzed, interpreted, and judged through the lenses of the elements of art and principles of design.

If we take time to seek understanding, relational thinking, we stand a better chance of creating places of authentic and meaningful learning. Or, putting it bluntly, as a teacher recently remarked: "I might obey you in your role as my supervisor, but you may only lead me when I know you as a person." I do not suggest that a supervisor has to make every teacher a best friend; however, I do mean a supervisor should break out of the hierarchical power relationships and seek lateral connective relationships. Yet, this requires distinguishing between inappropriate revelations and candor—a difficult line to navigate. In a recent article in the *Chronicle of Higher Education*, Stanley Fish (2004) wrote about the importance for administrators of practicing silence. Silence can be a powerful tool for developing trust and understanding. Regrettably, however, in many traditional school settings, school leaders want ultimate candor from teachers but will only expose minimal bits of information about themselves. It is a difficult and tricky dance. This formidable dance of human relationship is the challenge for truly successful schools. Authentic leadership in those settings resists becoming formulaic; rather, it is more about aesthetics. Here I speak of aesthetics not in the traditional conception of beauty but in Dewey's sense, of attention to the quality of nonverbal relationships. Attention to how nonverbal and nonsymbolic relationships create meaning is the art of human relations.

Many years after my experience with my art student, I began to study leadership from a practical and theoretical level. I began to believe that leadership was an art form. As a director of personnel and staff development I understood the budget demands, the costs of certified personnel, the state funding formula; it became clear that managing these competing demands was part of good, sound leadership. In observing principals and superintendents, I also saw how other factors (that is, vision and communication) contributed to successful leadership. In my many conversations with teachers, school board members, system administrators, principals, and community leaders, however, I became painfully aware that many people saw leadership as a stagnant, fixed set of attributes—a set of skills to apply to all situations at all times. Even more frightening was the assumption that some people were born to be leaders and others just were not so lucky. This last thought suggested that it might be a waste of time to engage some individuals, who did not have innate talents, in leadership development.

As my experience with my art student reminds me, art education is not only for those with "talent." Every child can learn the elements and principles of design—if not linguistically then certainly somatically. Art teachers are committed to this democratic vision of learning and have a distinctive toolkit for working on this problem. The question is, then, "What can leadership learn from this tool kit?"

When we view leadership narrowly, as a function of management and formula, we narrow our view of leadership from an art of human experience and understanding to a strategy for control and manipulation of personnel. I suggest that leadership is best described as "choreography of human understanding" and that by applying the language of art we can construct a lens through which the nature of our humanity begins to become clearer. At its most basic, the language of art begins with what are now called the elements of art and principles of design. Arthur Wesley Dow (1899; 1997) codified these elements and principles; artists continue to argue over the best way to conceptualize these ideas. For this study, I will work with seven elements and seven principles as advocated by Rozland Ragans in her textbook *Art Talk.*

I have as a fundamental belief that teaching is at its best when it is an art form. Accordingly, I also believe that supervision of teaching and leadership in schools must be based in aesthetics, the evaluation of art forms. It is against this arts-based backdrop that the writing emerges. I present in this book a methodology for describing, analyzing, interpreting, and evaluating school leadership and the supervision of teaching. Specifically, I will use the constructs of the elements of art and the principles of design as a vehicle for coming to terms with school leadership as art. The elements of art that I will use are line, value, shape, form, space, color, and texture. The principles of design that I suggest are emphasis, rhythm, movement, balance, proportion, variety, and harmony/unity.

In each school setting these fourteen attributes assume relative positions of importance. For example, it is very likely that at one school the element of texture might play a more prominent role than at another school, where shape or form may dominate. Although one element may be more obvious, all other elements are present, albeit to a lesser extent. In a different way, however, we will find that all principles might be present but that they do not always appear in any given setting. A school, for example, might adopt as one of its core values that it will make all decisions in light of the principle of proportion. Other principles of design may or may not be part of that adoption.

For the reader, allow me to set up what I have done in the chapters to follow. First, I offer fourteen original pieces of artwork from the collections of Joseph Norman. With each new element and with each new principle the reader will confront one of Joe's creations that capture the essential and key characteristics of the element or principle. I encourage the reader to pause, reflect on the definition and brief explanation, and then consider in what ways the art captures the element or the principle. There will likely be many elements and principles in the selections, but my choice serves to accentuate the topic of the moment.

So, the reader may anticipate that throughout the book I will offer an art form, define the element or principle, and then give an example from the art world. This rendering will help us begin the construction of meaning from a shared point of departure. I will thereafter offer a specific, real-life case study that embodies the key elements of a related issue in educational leadership. Finally, I will offer reflections on the possible implications that the concept has for the construction of the art of leadership.

In chapters 2 through 5 I will examine the school leadership function in the broadest sense. In particular, I will inspect notions of adult learning theory, effective communication, building management, personnel management, resource management, and several other noninstructional areas of managing the schooling process. In the latter chapters I will turn my attention toward the aesthetic evaluation of instructional supervision. In both sections, my examination will use the elements of art and principles of design as the conceptual constructs for aesthetic evaluation.

In chapter 1, I will construct a rationale for the use of art generally, and the elements and principles specifically, as a mode of understanding leadership and supervision. I provide there a conceptual basis for understanding leadership through the lens of Arts-Based Research. In chapter 2, I offer a sampling of alternative views of leadership and supervision and how writers have sought to define it and the potential limits of such definitions. Building on the language of visual art, the chapters following will offer alternative views and examples of leadership and develop an understanding through the application of Arts-Based Research.

Toward the ends of defining, evaluating, and thus understanding the leadership function, in chapter 3 I utilize the seven elements of line, shape, form, space, color, value, and texture. In chapter 4 I use the principles of design—emphasis, rhythm, movement, balance, proportion, variety, and harmony/unity. Using this format, I hope to move the reader quickly from theoretical considerations to concrete and specific applications in practice. The reader will

find suggested action plan formats in the appendixes for assessing elements
and principles (see appendixes B and C). In chapter 5 I attempt to bring the
pieces together into a holistic conversation about the "so what" of the elements
and principles and their contribution to understanding the complexities of
school leadership.

In the next chapters I will begin a more specific examination of leadership
within the context of instructional supervision. To help us see the differing
views of leadership versus supervision, I have included in chapters 7 and 8
the same scenarios as I did in chapters 3 and 4. By having the same scenarios I hope to make the distinctions between leadership and supervision,
when there are any, more conspicuous.

I offer a conceptual basis for supervision and evaluating it as an art form
in chapter 6. As in the first portion of the text, I use the elements to view supervision in chapter 7 and the principles of design in chapter 8. In chapter 9
I will collect the pieces of the supervision discussion into a final overview of
supervision as aesthetic practice. In chapter 10 I will summarize key findings
about the art of leadership and the art of supervision and comment on possible similarities and differences between the two. I will close my work with
some final thoughts and reflections.

This book will engage leadership through the relative interplay of the elements or art and principles of design and how they might inform us about
the leadership function. I envision that by using the language that the elements provide and coupling it with the organizing nature of the principles,
we can begin to grapple with the different images of leadership. As such, this
book is a practical application of the relatively new methodology of Arts-
Based Research to the field of educational leadership.

I hope the work can offer readers a chance to reflect on their own leadership style and the nature of their relationships, both personal and professional. A beginning point for such personal reflection might include a self-
analysis of readiness included in appendix D. I also hope that coming to
terms with the aesthetic nature of leadership our school leaders, both in the
classroom and in the front office, can enlarge their view of what effective
schools and teaching might look like. I believe that it is in the process of such
reflection that we can become more authentic and honest with ourselves and
with others. And I suggest that it is in the process of the aesthetic practice
that leadership takes on its most powerful art form.

1

Arts-Based Research Applied to Leadership: Elements and Principles of Design as a Forum for Conversation

One of the more frustrating matters for students when first asked to describe what they see in a painting is that they do not have a mechanism for conversation. They are not aware of, and therefore have no capacity for, the language of art. Ragans (1995), in her classroom text *Art Talk*, states:

> Each language has its own system of words and rules of grammar. To learn a new language you need to learn new words and a new set of rules for putting those words together.
> The language of visual art also has its own system. All of the objects you look at in a work of art are made up of certain common elements. They are arranged according to basic principles. As you learn these basic elements and principles, you will learn the language of art.
> Being able to use the language of visual art will help you in many ways. It will increase your ability to understand, appreciate, and enjoy art. It will increase your ability to express yourself clearly when discussing art. It will even help you improve your ability to produce artworks (p. 6).

If we can work from the assumption, then, that leadership is an art form and is best described as choreography of human understanding, we would do well to develop a mechanism for "seeing" it as an artist might view a painting or a choreographer a dance. That mechanism comes in the form of the elements of art and the principles of design. It is the goal of this book to help the reader begin developing some facility with aesthetic dimensions of school leadership.

The language of art that I am utilizing comes in the form of seven elements of art and seven principles of design. In each school setting and in each classroom, these fourteen attributes can assume different relative positions of importance. For example, it is very likely that at one school the leadership element

1

of texture plays a more prominent role than at another school, where shape or form may dominate. Whichever element is most obvious, all other elements are still present, albeit in a decreased stature.

Differently, not all seven principles are always evident in all leadership settings. Often one or more principles takes on a larger role than the remaining five or six principles. Different settings, different needs, different students, different communities, and different teachers all call for leadership decisions that are specific to particular places and times. This book defines and evaluates leadership through the relative interplay of the elements of art and the principles of design. By using the language that the elements provide and coupling it with the organizing nature of principles, we can begin to grapple with the different images of leadership.

If, then, we assume that leadership in its purest form is art, we are compelled to use the language of art, in the form of elements of art and principles of design, to come to understand the nature of the form. Eisner (1985) has explored the implications of this challenge most fully in his work *The Educational Imagination*. A few of the more notable scholars who also looked to the arts to provide useful models to better understand and improve educational practice are S. Lawrence-Lightfoot (1983; 1997), P. Jackson (1998), T. Barone (1998), and A. Blumberg (1989). Within art, I suggest that disciplines of aesthetics and criticism in general, and the Feldman method specifically (1995), provide us a structure for understanding.

Dewey (1934) conceived aesthetics as the branch of philosophy that allows us to analyze the way we look at the qualities of our world and assign value to our experiences. Dewey's aesthetics provides a theoretical construct for thinking about leadership. We are engaging in aesthetic thinking when we use our perceptions, sensations, and imagination to gain insight into what we might feel and understand about the world (Greene, 2001). Furthermore, Dewey (1934) implies that aesthetics refers to our first critical reflection on objects we experience. What is especially important is that our experiences stem from attention to qualitative relationships. Through these reflections our world and the wonder of life begin to take on deeper meaning. Priorities become clear. Important events assume an appropriate relationship with daily challenges. As these experiences first occur outside of language and our expected constructions of the world, they offer us opportunities for understanding by reflecting on them. Powerful experiences can help us reconstruct our world. This type of reflective analysis of experience is an integral part of critical theory through which we examine our own practice and habits of mind.

In cultivating this sensitivity we begin taking on an aesthetic task. We begin answering questions: What is of value? What is meaningful? What is moving about a given situation? It is through attending to the smallest nuances of art or life that we begin to ascend to a more attentive form of existence. We move to a plane of existence that releases imagination, passions, curiosity, and extraordinary circumstances. It is Dewey's view of reflection that leads us to the notion of critical theory as a vehicle for understanding and valuing. Dewey was adamant that this form of aesthetic experience as antithetical to the appreciation of beauty. Dewey's aesthetics is an active form or mental engagement with the world—not a detached, coldly objective appraisal.

When we recognize that leadership is inseparable from human interaction, we begin to understand that leadership is more about listening to and understanding each other than devising a checklist of behaviors. It is engagement, not detachment or mere observation. The benefit is that we begin to appreciate the nuances and subtleties that come with managing and leading people. Being able to engage in this critique of human interaction and motivation allows us to view leadership as an art rather than a formula. I have come to imagine, in fact, that leadership is metaphorically a "Dance of Understanding." It is interpretative, relative, and sophisticated. As such, it requires a comparable methodology for understanding: aesthetics, critical theory, and leadership as art.

THE FELDMAN METHOD AS AESTHETICS AND CRITICAL THEORY

Edmund Feldman, an art professor for many years at the University of Georgia, has provided generations of artists with a paradigm for art criticism. His four-step (description, analysis, interpretation, judgment) approach offers students a specific process for undertaking aesthetics or critical theory. Take a moment to observe the Feldman Method in the example on pages 4 and 5. First are the categories or steps of the process. The second portion prompts us with questions about the nature of our observation. The third section provides us a place to make notes, reactions, or observations. I think it is notable that the first two categories really emphasize delaying judgments and spending energy rather than describing what we see and beginning to discern the presence of elements of art and principles of design. In the latter categories, we are prompted to begin making decisions and judgments about our observation. For many of us who have spent a professional career understanding teaching and learning, there is a interesting parallel between the artists who use the Feldman Method and teachers who use Bloom's (Anderson, 2001) Taxonomy for Learning Objectives (i.e., knowledge, comprehension, application, analysis, synthesis, evaluation) or instructional supervisors who use Fuller's (1969) Stages of Concern Theory (awareness, information, personal, management, consequence, collaboration, refocusing). In all these cases there is a linear, developmental construction of knowledge and understanding. There is a real and authentic engagement and thus the experience becomes aesthetic in nature. Following, I offer the Feldman method and after each step a sample of what an observer might determine or imagine regarding one of Joseph Norman's works.

Title: "Nocturnes for Heather"
Artist: Joseph Norman
Medium: Ink wash on paper
Date: 1996

Step 1: Description
Goal is to describe objectively what you see; to delay judgment. List title; artist; date; medium; size. Is work representational, abstract, or
nonobjective? Can you identify a subject? If not, are there objective
"hints" about a subject? Describe how the elements are used.
A description might include: Joseph Norman, 1996; "Nocturnes for
Heather," 24 × 19 in.; Ink wash on paper; still life of a vase, with flowers and leaves, black and white with values of gray, values create

forms, dark spaces create shapes of leaves, lighter spaces create positive space.

Step 2: Analysis

Goal is to describe behaviors of what you see. Describe how the elements above use the principles of design. And identify the feelings that the elements and principles engender.

The analysis might include: Create moodiness through use of dark and light, especially a sense of mystery. Joyfulness is also present. Forms and shapes create fullness. Negative and positive spaces work to remove some of the mystery.

Step 3: Interpretation

Goal is to find meaning in what you see. How do features and qualities that you have observed combine to create meaning? What does the work remind you of? Why? What do you think the artist is trying to do? What is the intended use of the object? Are there symbols in the work? What do they mean?

One interpretation might be: Vase and flowers suggest feminine quality. The vegetation is full of life. There is music and dancing, emphasized by movement of vegetation. There is emphasis on the female form, particularly in the notion of the vase. The vase holds the water that provides sustaining life to the dance of the flowers.

Step 4: Judgment

Goal: To evaluate what you see. Does the work have value through formal qualities (use of elements and principles of design)? Value through expression of emotion or feeling? Value through purpose? Are materials appropriate? How could it have been more successful? Who might value this work?

A possible judgment would include: The use of metaphor is powerful and appropriate. Movement, mystery, joy, symmetry, and balance work together to build unity and wholeness, much as we might hope for in a new and exciting relationship. There is even the suggestion of fullness and color through the black and white shades suggesting that we remember to rely on the common, everyday occurrences to bring life and color to our relationships.

When I transform the Feldman Method, however, from a mechanism of critiquing art to a mechanism for critiquing the art of leadership, I begin to transform my understandings and assumptions of the whole leadership function. The basic format is the same: I have four categories; I have suggestions or prompts for consideration; and I have opportunities for making notes and observations. Some of what appears below might at first be a bit unclear. That discomfort is expected because only after working through the remaining pages will readers begin to develop some skills in using the elements and principles. Nevertheless, I offer the following concrete and specific example for reference. In the Leadership Critique, we might approach the study this way:

Topic/Issue at Hand: Summer Staff Development Planning
Leader Name: Central Office Person
School/System Setting: Independent School #1
Date: 2004

Step 1: Description
The goal is to describe objectively what you see; to delay judgment. List system, leader, date; describe setting and key players; identify central or core issue; identify elements of leadership that are present.
A description might include: I have located the staff development plan for the district. The district has 5,000 students and 350 certified teachers, one high school, one middle school, seven elementary schools. Line, shape, form are present; 10 people (one from each school and one from central office) are on the staff development planning team.

Step 2: Analysis
The goal is to describe behaviors of what you see. Describe how the elements listed in step 1 use the principles of leadership. Which principles provide organization for the elements? List your emotional reaction to these factors. How does the leadership strategy make you feel? How does it make others feel?
The analysis might include: Lack of line makes it unclear which decisions are open to negotiation and discussion and which are not. Shape: entire energy in meetings seems to be on managing budget and scheduling summer schedule. Form is absent, as little opportunity for hearing others or seeing other perspectives is encouraged. No principle seems to be at work. Frustration, annoyance, and low energy are present. No clear leadership strategy is at work.

Step 3: Interpretation
The goal is to find meaning in what you see. Does it work? Why? What do you think the leader is trying to do? What is the goal? What are the symbolic goals that emerge? What do they mean?
One interpretation might be: The group is clearly frustrated by a lack of progress or focus. Several commented among themselves that the same thing happened every time but little was ever accomplished. Central Office person is attempting to control decisions. Others are invited into decisions on staff development, but clearly shared decision making is not encouraged.

Step 4: Judgment

The goal is to evaluate what you see. How could the leader have been more successful? Who benefits from the decisions? Who does not? What balance is there between what the leader says, what he does, and what he believes? What is the relationship between what the school values, believes, and does?

A possible judgment would include: If the leader had been more explicit about what was negotiable and what was not (e.g., line), the rules would have been clearer and participants would not have been so frustrated. Managing time and money (e.g., shape) could have been placed at a later meeting after decisions based on needs of students had been made. The biggest problem lies in the fact that the teachers did not believe their ideas were of value (e.g., form). A real disconnect between what is said about values and what is practiced (sharing vs. controlling). Group or leader must commit to a principle so that all decisions can be guided through that "filter."

ELEMENTS AND PRINCIPLES APPLIED TO A CRITIQUE OF LEADERSHIP

Following the guidance of aesthetics, critical theory, and the Feldman Method, we can view art through the lenses of the elements of art and principles of design. The elements and principles provide art observers with a language for critique.

Borrowing this notion from the world of art, I will use the elements to describe specific, observable attributes of the art of leadership. The elements are line, shape, form, space, color, value, and texture. In terms of understanding leadership, I suggest that the elements will offer building blocks for understanding basic leadership skills. In some settings, all the elements might be at work. In other instances, only selected elements will come to bear on managing and leading.

I take each of the elements as discrete parts of the leadership function. As we become more skilled at describing leadership, we will also notice that it is difficult and artificial to see the elements as "stand alone" skills of leadership. Rather, the reality is more about one element playing a primary role while other elements function in a supportive capacity. Together, they support the leader's ability to work through a given situation.

The principles represent the guiding laws or organizing strategies for constructing different effects and meaning in art. In matters of principle, the art observer asks questions relative to emphasis, rhythm, movement, balance, proportion, variety, and harmony/unity. I will use the principles to create philosophical and thematic constructs for leadership in schools. Just as we can put words together to make a sentence (elements = words) we can put together sentences to construct a descriptive narrative (principles = sentences).

As we rely on elements and principles of design, we begin to come to terms with what we see, feel, and sense. Understanding leadership becomes an aesthetic process. We not only know it cognitively and conceptually but also emotionally and personally—and leadership is skill, emotional and personal.

If we assume that leadership, when it is done well, is an art, then applying the standards of the seven elements and seven principles of design might help us to begin to know what leadership does, what it looks like, what it feels like, what makes it work. Just as with art, school leadership is not about finding a "magic formula." There are certainly essential components of effective leadership, and the elements discussion will clarify this issue. It is the study of principle, however, that helps bring the elements together in different ways for different people in an ever-changing world.

Given the complexity of people and situations that leaders confront, it is no small wonder that no prescription exists. But, when we see something work at this school or that system, we often try to assign the success to a single strategy or individual. The reality is, however, that the success comes from the interdependence and interaction of several leadership functions—in much the same way that the elements and principles might contribute to the interpretation of an artwork.

QUESTIONS FOR DISCUSSION

1. Select your favorite painting and try to find which elements and principles are present.
2. Select your favorite painting and apply the Feldman Method to critique the work. Remember, don't talk about what you like or don't like. It is important to suspend judgment and describe just what you see.
3. Take the Art of Leadership Critique (appendix A) and apply to it the leadership of a national, regional, or local leader. Suspend judgment and describe what you see.
4. Apply the Leadership Critique to an event in your school.
5. How might using the Leadership Critique be used to help a local business improve customer service?
6. Reflect on your personal life and apply the Leadership Critique to your own experiences. Use the chart as a device for personal reflection and growth. Also, use appendix D to assess your growth.

2

Reflections on the Nature of Leadership

One of the essential elements of leadership is the ability to prioritize amid competing demands. School leadership's ability to distinguish between what is immediate and what is really important can be lifesaving, not to mention professionally rewarding. When we in school leadership allow the multiple events that confront us to set the agenda for our days, we begin to lose control over our days. We become victim to the events of the day instead of being in charge of the day. We become what Conner (1992) characterized as an event-driven mentality. The alternative, however, for leadership is to be clear about what matters most and to allow decisions and priorities to emerge from that assumption. This type of approach might be more appropriately called core-values driven (Conner, 1992). Focus and clarity about our values are possible when we provide opportunities for both personal and organizational reflection.

DEFINING LEADERSHIP

There are several issues associated with understanding the concept of leadership. First, we often struggle to assign a single, fixed set of characteristics to leadership. An alternative approach might be to understand leadership more fully as within a constellation of attributes. Admittedly, if we could "fix" on one set, we would likely have an easier time training people to be good leaders; at least, it might be simpler to understand why some people are successful leaders and others are not. The concept of leadership, however, is in many ways relational. In other words, the actions of an individual might support the notion of leadership in a given scenario, but those same characteristics might not be celebrated as effective in a different setting. Consider for

9

a moment the army general who leads a force to victory in World War II. That same person, using those same skills, might not have the same level of success leading a business or school. We are finding this same sort confusion with many school districts as boards of education hire successful business executives as superintendents. It is not yet clear that the skills that helped the executives be successful in the private sector are applicable to schools. Sergiovanni maintains that the attempt to apply private, business models to public schools is in fact evidence of a gross misunderstanding of the nature and purpose of schooling. Putting it directly, when we apply business models to a social institution (e.g., schools) we misunderstand the essential elements and assumptions found in both models.

A final difficulty in coming to terms with the notion of leadership is that by its very nature leadership is an abstraction but may be supported by concrete actions. In other words, the actions are symptoms of leadership, not leadership itself. Take two principals who have the capacity to stay calm amid competing demands. For the one principal, being calm might be a matter of seeing things from a set of core values that guide all decisions. This type of groundedness might be symptomatic of good leadership. Take the other principal, however, and we might find that staying calm is a function of being frozen by choices. The principal seems calm but in fact is simply incapable of motion, because he has no idea of what to do next. Outwardly, the principals show symptoms of effective leadership. Inwardly, there are very different things going on. So, finding a list of what makes for effective leadership can be helpful but is clearly insufficient to understanding the complex and often abstract notion of leadership.

CRITERIAL VERSUS NONCRITERIAL ATTRIBUTES OF LEADERSHIP

Now that we have established that understanding the nature of leadership is at best an elusive goal, we can either just give up the pursuit or acknowledge the challenge and move ahead. To move ahead, let us carry the idea of leadership as a concept a bit further by being clear about conceptual development and understanding.

Writing about concept acquisition within the context of social studies teaching and learning, Martorella (1985) promotes the notion that criterial attributes are the essential properties that define a concept. For example, given the concept of a school, we might define it as a place where learning and teaching happen. We might also note that a school is often a certain type of building where teachers instruct and students come to learn. While both descriptions are important and helpful, only the first one is necessary. It is often the case that a school is a building, but it is clearly not always necessary for a school to have a building. Consider the many types of scientific labs that become schools in the field, not schools in the building. The specific physical structure of a school is a noncriterial attribute in that it is often character-istic but not a sine qua non of a school. Another example that helps clarify the differences might be found in considering a museum. Learning and teaching can certainly take place at a museum and thus qualify it in an es-sential sense as a school. But the museum will very likely not have the same appearance or attendance pattern of a more traditional school setting. So when we begin to decide what a school is, to be accurate we must be cer-tain what is essential and necessary versus what is not.

Another way to think about this discussion of attributes is the concept of stereotypes. Stereotypes help us "order" our lives by giving us consistent rules for making sense of our world. Although the term "stereotype" can con-note negative images, the real danger is not in having stereotypes but stereo-types that are not open to examination. For example, if we were to ask a student what an American Indian might look like, the student might offer a picture of a warrior with headdress riding a horse bareback. Although we might be offended by such a simplistic and singular understanding, we would do well to help that student understand that his stereotype can be en-larged and redefined to embrace a more accurate view of what an American Indian might look like. The student assumed that the criterial elements of the American Indian were headdress and horseback riding. Although those ele-ments might be important, they are not sufficient to define the culture of what makes an American Indian. As is often the case, the student has gener-alized an understanding that was only specific to a certain type of person in a particular time to represent an entire culture across all time.

Given this distinction between criterial and noncriterial attributes and the danger associated with fixed stereotypes, I began to imagine what might be the essential, necessary elements of effective leadership. What might be the attributes that can be generalized to most settings and people or might have applications beyond one place and time? To my way of thinking, we cannot find the answer in a static list. Rather, I suggest that we engage in this pursuit much as the artist might engage a work of visual art. There are specific, quantified elements and principles of effective leadership, but their interpretation and application are dependent on context and on the ob-server. Maybe by calling on the artist's perspective, I can offer a language that communicates the art of what makes for an effective leader, one that helps distinguish between criterial and noncriterial conceptions.

HOW SELECTED WRITERS HAVE DEFINED LEADERSHIP

The educational leadership community, business leaders, athletics coaches, philosophers, and others have developed a broad view of what might make for effective leaders. At times the lists seem endless, but certainly we find many commonalities embedded in those list. It would serve us well to consider, if only for a moment, what writers from a variety of backgrounds have determined were criterial attributes of effective leadership.

Although his work is somewhat dated, Stephen R. Covey (1989) continues to offer popular culture a way to define leadership generally in his *Seven Habits of Highly Effective People*. For Covey, leadership has both private and public dimensions; as individuals become more comfortable with those notions, they become better leaders of themselves and subsequently of others. His list includes:

Private Victory

1. Be proactive: Principles of personal vision
2. Begin with the end in mind: Principles of personal leadership
3. Put first things first: Principles of personal management.

Public Victory

1. Think win/win: Principles of interpersonal leadership
2. Seek first to understand . . . then to be understood: Principles of empathetic communication
3. Synergize: Principles of creative cooperation
4. Sharpen the Saw: Principles of balanced renewal.

Another popular spokesman for leadership is John C. Maxwell. Having written some twenty-five books about leadership and how individuals might cultivate successful leadership traits within themselves, Maxwell (1998) gives us yet another list in his *The 21 Irrefutable Laws of Leadership*:

1. Leadership ability determines a person's level of effectiveness.
2. The true measure of leadership is influence—nothing more, nothing less.
3. Leadership develops daily, not in a day.
4. Anyone can steer the ship, but it takes a leader to chart the course.
5. When the real leader speaks, people listen.
6. Trust is the foundation of leadership.
7. People naturally follow leaders stronger than themselves.
8. Leaders evaluate everything with a leadership bias.
9. Who you are is who you attract.
10. Leaders touch a heart before they ask for a hand.
11. A leader's potential is determined by those closest to him.
12. Only secure leaders give power to others.
13. It takes a leader to raise up a leader.
14. People buy into the leader, then the vision.
15. Leaders find a way for the team to win.
16. Momentum is a leader's best friend.
17. Leaders understand that activity is not necessarily accomplishment.

18. A leaders must give up to go up.
19. When to lead is as important as what to do and where to go.
20. To add growth, lead followers—to multiply, lead leaders.
21. A leader's lasting value is measured by succession.

Drawing on an extensive research project into everyday actions and behaviors of exemplary leaders at all levels in a variety of settings, James Kouzes and Barry Posner (1995), in their book *The Leadership Challenge: How to Keep Getting Extraordinary Things Done in Organizations* (2nd edition), argue that successful leaders have five common practices:

1. Challenging the process: Searching for opportunities, experimenting
2. Inspiring a shared vision: Envisioning the future, enlisting others
3. Enabling others to act: Strengthening others, fostering collaboration
4. Modeling the way: Setting an example, planning the small wins
5. Encouraging the heart: Recognizing contributions, celebrating accomplishments.

Kouzes and Posner also note that the leadership characteristics that most often attract followers are:

1. Honesty
2. Competence
3. Vision
4. Inspiration
5. Credibility.

Warren Bennis and Burt Nanus (1997) in *Leaders: Strategies for Taking Charge* (2nd edition), concluded that effective leaders share the following leadership traits:

1. Vision
2. The ability to develop trust through effective communication
3. Persistence
4. Avidity to learn.

Marcus Buckingham and Curt Coffman (1999), in *First, Break All the Rules: What the World's Greatest Managers Do Differently,* suggest that great managers follow three steps:

1. Define right outcomes.
2. Tell employees what you want but let them choose how to get there.
3. Focus on strengths. The best managers focus on talents and manage around the weaknesses.

In 1992 Daryl R. Conner wrote his view of leadership in light of relentless demands of change in *Managing at the Speed of Change: How Resilient Managers Succeed and Prosper Where Others Fail.* Of particular importance to Conner was that leadership is a function of staying focused on the core mission amid a storm of change and competing demands. Specifically, "effective leaders are capable of reframing the thinking of those whom they guide, enabling them to see that significant changes are not only imperative but achievable" (p. 9). The way that leaders can be resilient in the face of change is to:

1. Display a sense of security and self-assurance that is based on their view of life as complex but filled with opportunity (Positive).
2. Have a clear vision of what they want to achieve (Focused).
3. Demonstrate a special pliability when responding to uncertainty (Flexible).
4. Develop structured approaches to managing ambiguity (Organized).
5. Engage change rather than defend against it (Proactive).

In his *On Leadership,* John Gardner (1990) usefully distinguishes between leaders/managers and managers. Although both have important functions to support the organization, only one is truly a leader, according to Gardner. Leader/managers distinguish themselves in at least six respects:

1. They think longer-term—beyond the day's crises, beyond the quarterly report, beyond the horizon.
2. In thinking about the unit they are heading, they grasp its relationship to larger realities.
3. They reach and influence constituents beyond their jurisdictions, beyond boundaries.
4. They put heavy emphasis on the tangibles of vision, values, and motivation, and they understand intuitively the nonrational and unconscious elements in leader/constituent interaction.
5. They have the political skill to cope with the conflicting requirements of multiple constituencies.
6. They think in terms of renewal (p. 4).

In popular circles, many authors, like the ones listed above, have coupled their writings on leadership development with a sort of personal self-help approach. Indeed, there is value in such writings, as they help readers begin to reflect on values, on perspectives, on what matters most. In the educational world, however, leadership development focuses more on how we might create places where students can learn deeply and well. Some of the most important educational writers have devoted their lives to articulating views of the successful school leader. More recently, there has emerged a growing emphasis on creating teacher-leaders. But the fundamental pursuit remains: What does effective leadership look like in our schools? And in an equally relevant vein: How can leadership development in our schools support student achievement? Below, I offer a sampling of some of the educational community's answer to these questions.

In her *Leadership Capacity for Lasting School Improvement*, Linda Lambert (2003) writes that leadership is a "combination of breadth of participation and depth of skillfulness" (p. 4) and that the interplay of that balance creates different patterns of leadership capacity in schooling. She imagines school-level leadership as having basically four dimensions: low degree of skill, high degree of skill, low degree of participation, high degree of participation.

In particular, Lambert notes that when leadership has a low degree of skill combined with a low degree of participation, the school is characterized in the following ways:

- Principal as autocratic manager
- One-way flow of information; no shared vision
- Codependent, paternal/maternal relationships; rigidly defined roles
- Norms of compliance and blame; technical and superficial program coherence
- Little innovation in teaching and learning
- Poor student achievement or only short-term improvements on standardized tests.

When school leadership is characterized by a low degree of skill but with a high degree of participation, then one can find:

- Principal as "laissez-faire" manager, many teachers developing unrelated programs
- Fragmented information that lacks coherence; programs that lack shared purpose
- Norms of individualism; no collective responsibility
- Undefined roles and responsibilities
- "Spotty" innovation; some classrooms are excellent while others are poor
- Static overall student achievement (unless data are disaggregated).

When leadership capacity is described as having a high degree of skill but a low degree of participation, Lambert describes these schools as:

- Principal and key teachers as purposeful leadership team
- Limited use of schoolwide data; information flow within designated leadership groups

- Polarized staff with pockets of strong resistance
- Efficient designated leaders; others serve in traditional roles
- Strong innovation, reflection skills, and teaching excellence; weak program coherence
- Student achievement is static or shows slight improvement.

Finally, Lambert notes that school leadership described as having both high skill and high degree of participation typically are described as:

- Principal, teachers, parents, and students as skillful leaders
- Shared vision resulting in program coherence
- Inquiry-based use of data to inform decisions and practice
- Broad involvement, collaboration, and collective responsibility reflected in roles and actions
- Reflective practice that leads consistently to innovation
- High or steadily improving student achievement.

Jerry Patterson (1998) observed that effective leaders were those who could remain resilient in the face of adversity. Building on Conner's work noted above, Patterson identifies eight strengths of resilient leaders:

Strength #1: Be Positive in Spite of Adversity

- Expect the world to be filled with disruptions.
- Seek opportunities instead of obstacles.
- Think *How Can We?* rather than *We Can't.*

Strength #2: Stay Focused on What You Care About

- Maintain a strong sense of purpose and vision.
- Buffer others from unnecessary distractions.
- Maintain perspective for the long haul.

Strength #3: Remain Flexible in How You Get There

- Develop a high tolerance for ambiguity.
- Recover quickly from setbacks.
- Learn how to work within imposed constraints.
- Be willing to see diverse perspectives.

Strength #4: Organize Your Energy to Move Ahead

- Identify what's important in apparently confusing conditions.
- Learn how to successfully manage competing demands.

- Know where to go for support and resources.
- Don't waste energy on resilience-draining issues.

Strength #5: Act Rather than React

- Recognize when change is inevitable.
- Take risks in spite of potentially adverse consequences.
- Improvise new approaches to move ahead during adversity.

Strength #6: Create a Climate of Caring and Support

- Help everyone in the school feel cared for and supported.
- Develop creative incentives, recognition, and rewards.
- Secure resources for nurturing in the face of adversity.

Strength #7: Maintain High Expectations for Success

- Create a schoolwide belief that everyone can succeed in adverse conditions.
- Hold firmly to high standards even during tough times.
- Don't use adversity as an excuse for becoming a victim.

Strength #8: Create Meaningful Participation

- View everyone as a resource rather than as a problem.
- Invite nay-sayers into the conversation about moving ahead.
- Seize the school's collective energy to overcome adversity.

Lee G. Bolman and Terrence E. Deal (1995), in *Leading with Soul,* represent a growing body of research that embraces the affective element of leadership. For them, leadership is as much a matter of disposition as skill and content development. Utilizing a literary form emphasizing conversations, Bolman and Deal offer the reader an important distinction between the leader as the "heroic champion" and as "policy wonk." But for these authors, these two versions of leadership "emphasize the hands and heads of leaders, neglecting the deeper and more enduring elements of courage, spirit, and hope" (p. 5). Moving from managing to leading might be simply a focus on:

1. Heart
2. Hope
3. Faith
4. Introspection
5. Ethics
6. Spiritual centering.

Thomas J. Sergiovanni (2000) suggests that school leadership is more about stewardship than about managing and controlling. "The leadership that counts, in the end, is the kind that touches people differently. It taps their emotions, appeals to their values, and responds to their connections with other people. It is a morally based leadership—a form of stewardship" (p. 270). His view of servant leadership, albeit abbreviated here, might be captured by practicing:

1. Purposing: The process by which the staff builds within the school a center of shared values that transforms it from a mere organization into a covenantal community.
2. Empowerment: Everyone is free to do what makes sense, as long as people's decisions embody the values shared by the school community.
3. Leadership by Outrage: It is the leader's responsibility to be outraged when empowerment is abused and when purposes are ignored. Moreover, all members of the school community are obliged to show outrage when the standard falls.

Carl Glickman, Stephen Gordon, and Jovita Ross-Gordon, in their 2004 edition of *SuperVision and Instructional Leadership: A Developmental Approach,* call for a paradigm shift in supervision. They base much of their work on Gordon's 1997 research findings that instructional leadership, or supervision, includes:

1. A collegial rather than hierarchical relationship between teachers and formally designated supervisors.
2. Supervision as the province of teachers as well as formally designated supervisors.
3. A focus on teacher growth rather than teacher compliance.
4. Facilitation of teachers collaborating with each other in instructional improvement efforts.
5. Teacher involvement in ongoing reflective inquiry.

Glickman and colleagues have observed that leadership has moved from the principal's office to the classroom. Thus leadership becomes more a function of teacher leaders sharing in concerns, developing plans for improvement, and participating in evaluating as critical friends. Leadership can be measured, then, in relation to its support of student achievement. Outside of such evidence, there is little support for the notion of successful supervision.

In his 2003 work, *Centering Educational Administration: Cultivating Meaning, Community, and Responsibility,* Robert J. Starratt, one who has consistently supported the notion that leadership is above all else ethical, presents some basic elements of leadership:

1. It is grounded in basic meanings about human persons, society, knowledge, human development, the natural world, and schooling.
2. It is energized by a dramatic vision of what education might and should be.
3. It involves the articulation of that vision and the invitation to others to articulate a communal vision of schooling.
4. It seeks to embody the vision in the institutional mission, goals, policies, programs, and organizational structures.
5. It celebrates the vision in ordinary and special activities and seeks a continuous renewal of both the vision and its embodiment.

In 2004, Starratt positioned ethical leadership more succinctly as he maintained that quality leadership is a function of being responsible, authentic, and present. In developing these virtues, he asserts:

> Administrators, teachers, and students engage the work of the school as human beings, as learners and teachers, and as members of a civic community. These roles interpenetrate and enrich one another as the work of schooling progresses. Thus we treat the exercise of responsibility as a human being, as a learner or teacher, and as a member of the civic community; the exercise of authenticity as a human being, as a learner or teacher, and as a member of the civic community; and the exercise of presence as a human being, as a learner or teacher, and as a member of the civic community. The virtues of responsibility, authenticity, and presence interpenetrate and enrich one another. They need one another for their fullest exercise (p. 9).

Edward Pajak (2003), in his important work on instructional leadership, offers a leadership style that emphasizes the varying and complicated interplay between teaching styles and styles of supervision. For Pajak, instructional leadership might be based on a clinical model, an artistic/humanistic model, technical/didactic model, or a developmental/reflective model. Similarly, teaching styles might be based on a model of the knowing teacher, the caring teacher, the inventing teacher, or the inspiring teacher. The key to successful instructional leadership is rooted in the leader's ability "make a deliberate effort to honor and legitimate perspectives and practices that differ from their own preferred styles of perceiving, judging, and communicating about reality" (p. 4).

CONCLUSIONS ON THE ART OF LEADERSHIP

Above, I have offered a sampling of perspectives on leadership. Some of the references are based in educational settings while others are more general in coming to terms with what makes for an effective leader. At the very least, a quick review helps inform us that no one is particularly right or wrong. But what does occur is an emerging notion that leadership is thematic, philosophical, varying, sometimes case-specific, other times applicable to all settings. I suggest that by pursuing the artistic path to understanding effective leadership, one that emphasizes the art of human relations, we might come closer to synthesizing the elements and principles of school leadership.

QUESTIONS FOR DISCUSSION

1. Reflect on people in your life who have been important to your personal and professional development. What are the personal characteristics that describe your view of them?
2. List three to five people who you think are successful leaders. What characteristics do they share? In what ways are they different?
3. Who at your school do you consider successful leaders? What makes them successful?
4. What are the most important interpersonal traits of successful leaders?
5. What is the difference between managing and leading?
6. When is managing best and when is leading best?
7. What do you consider criterial attributes of effective leaders? What are some noncriterial attributes?

3

Using the Elements to Describe Leadership

The elements of art are the basic visual symbols in the language of art. They provide a specific, and often concrete, vocabulary for describing art. The elements are line, value, shape, form, space, color, and texture.

For leadership, the elements help us create a view, a perception, and a vision of leading. Within each school, all seven elements may be present. The relative perceptivity of the various elements in a school, however, can be very different, depending on changing needs, varying times of the year, or changes within the district. The constant, however, is that in effective schools, and by association in effective leadership, the seven elements provide a concrete, specific, and often daily chart for navigating the often difficult choices that come with educating our children for successful citizenship.

UNTITLED, *AUTUMN ONYX*, 2000

From the series "Tiergarten Variations"
Graphite on paper, 9 × 14 in.
Collection of the artist

Element No. 1

Line: A long narrow mark or stroke made on or in a surface.

The Artist's View

Artists recognize the important contribution line brings to a holistic understanding of a given work. Lines can be vertical, horizontal, diagonal,

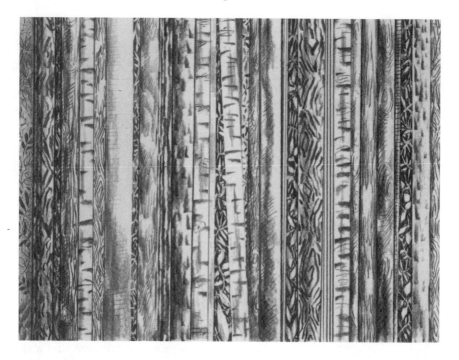

curvilinear, or zigzagged. When artists vary the line's length, width, texture, direction, or degree of curve they can multiply the visual impact of a work of art. For example, vertical lines convey height and inactivity. Vertical lines also express stability, dignity, poise, stiffness, and formality. Imagine how vertical lines on the side of a building will make the building look taller, more stable. By contrast, horizontal lines are static. They express peace, rest, quiet, and stability. Horizontal lines can help make one feel content, relaxed, and calm. Diagonal and zigzag lines suggest activity. They communicate action, movement, and tension. Diagonal lines also seem to work against gravity and create a pull and tension that can be uncomfortable. Curved lines also express activity. Spiral curves around a central point are hypnotic and tend to draw the eye to the center. Zigzag lines in an artwork help to create a feeling of confusion. Clearly an element as simple as a line can have a powerful effect on the message of a work of art.

Line as a Case Study

The principal at Sharing Elementary School wants to implement shared decision making with her staff. She has come to believe that by doing so she can support the site-based planning that the central office values as a part of the accreditation process. More specifically, the principal recognizes that shared decision making would be an important part of the school improvement plan. The question arises, however, of where to begin with this process.

The principal decides first to convene an interview committee for selecting new teachers. She asks that teacher leaders from each grade level select two representatives for the committee. One member is the primary participant, while the other is the alternate. The teachers are excited about this opportunity to be involved in an important part of the school's business. The interview team meets with the personnel director for legal guidelines and to develop an appropriate list of interview questions. The personnel office forwards applications for the committee's review. The committee selects five teachers for a formal interview.

The interviews go as scheduled. The teachers have open conversations about the merits of particular candidates in light of other candidates, and so on. Finally, the team makes the tough decision to hire a certain teacher. The committee forwards the selection to the principal. Several days later, at an open board meeting, the superintendent recommends to the board a different teacher to receive a contract. Word gets back to the interview committee. The teachers demand to see the principal.

Upon meeting the principal, the team discovers that the principal had selected the group to help with interviews but had felt no obligation to follow its recommendation. In fact, the principal thought the team's choice was a poor one; that was why she had recommended someone else. The teachers leave the meeting frustrated and demoralized. What had once seemed to be an open opportunity for shared decision making became another moment when the distance between the principal's office and the teachers' rooms exceeded the physical space.

In this scenario, the fault is not that the principal made the decision. Nor is it unrealistic for the teachers to be angered. What was missing in the process was an honest discussion about the role of the interview team in the selection process. If the principal did not feel obligated to accept the team's recommendation, that was certainly reasonable. The team did not understand the negotiable lines, the boundaries and limits of its mission, and the force of its resulting decisions. If the teachers had known that their recommendation was only that, a recommendation, the nature of the relationship would have been clear. The team would have known what was expected. They could have appreciated the invitation to be a part of the decision making while realizing that ultimately the principal would make the decision regarding employment matters.

A Leadership Perspective

For school leaders, "line" means to be clear about boundaries and parameters. Successful school leaders communicate expectations for students and staff. They act in ways consistent with that understanding. Few things are as demoralizing to a staff as to see the leader applying rules inconsistently. The

school draws stability, dignity, and poise from the consistent and fair application of rules and expectations.

Line also serves to remind leadership of the important role of mission and vision. When teachers are clear about where the school is going and how it is going to get there, they begin to understand their role in the process. Conversely, when the direction of the school seems flat, or horizontal, then the learning atmosphere becomes stagnant and unproductive.

Finally, line informs leadership about the boundaries between the negotiable and the nonnegotiable. If a school committee is to decide a particular issue, effective leadership is clear about what is open to conversation and what is not. For a committee to work at an issue and submit a solution only to discover that its answer was not one of the options can frustrate good intentions.

TARGET PRACTICE NO. 3, 1994

From the series "Target Practice Take This Take That"
Charcoal on paper, 50 × 40 in.
Collection of Museum of Fine Arts, Boston, MA
Gift of Dr. and Mrs. Joseph A. Chazan

Element No. 2

Value: The lightness or darkness of a color or object.

The Artist's View

Value is the art element that describes the relative darkness or lightness of an object in a drawing or painting. How much value a surface has is dependent on how much light is reflected. If there is an absence of light, the surface will be dark; if there is much light, the surface becomes lighter. There are many ways in which artists create value. For example, when one looks at a dollar bill, one may see an entire artwork that is composed of tiny lines. The artist or the engraver uses lines to create value. The closer and more plentiful the lines in a space, the darker the value. In turn, the less line in a given space the less value, and the space appears lighter. In fact, value is related to all the elements and is often understood best in association with other elements.

Value as a Case Study

At Florence High School, the principal, Mike Angelo, proclaims that the arts are a central focus for creating productive citizens. He did a PowerPoint presentation at the last PTO meeting where he talked about arts in the school. Just this morning, however, Mr. Angelo received a memo from the district finance director that he was to cut next year's school budget by 5 percent. Also, based on recent directives from the state education department, all principals were to place special emphasis on the basics. The superintendent stated, "Student test scores simply must improve or we will be placed on probation and we do not need that publicity!"

Mr. Angelo calls in Mr. Drum, Ms. Shakespeare, and Ms. Pallette and informs them that since they all have less than three years' experience in the district, he will have to let them go at the end of the year. When Ms. Pallette, the art teacher, asks why Mr. Gridiron, who has been with the system only two years, is not being released, the principal states, "The community is not going to tolerate losing the football coach, who just returned from an exciting college experience at Football A&M. Anyway, he is one of Florence High's most famous graduates."

When we say that we value academics and the arts but our actions communicate something very different, the message is lost. In essence, our articulated values are inconsistent with our daily practices. This type of disconnect can destroy teacher morale, communicate dangerous messages to students, and confuse our purpose for schooling. The light of our message becomes lost behind the shadows of our actions. Although the example is ridiculous at one level, many of us know of examples that echo this story.

A Leadership Perspective

For school leadership, value represents the "light" that emerges from our daily activities, which reflect our attention to what matters most. Often in schools we fail to recognize, or to remember, what is most important. We earnestly engage in any number of activities that seem important for the moment but that cast little light on the picture of what we are. In other words, our actions do not adequately support our most central, core values.

Core values are not observations, perceptions, or operating rules. They are things we believe to be extremely important. They are characterized by such descriptors as "fundamental," "guiding," "philosophical," "pointing the way." Core values help answer such questions as: Who are we? What do we stand for? What business are we really in? What is important to us? Where do we want to go in our preferred future?

Accompanying core values are "We will" statements. "We will" statements are specific, concrete, observable, measurable actions that support the philosophy that emerges from core values. In many instances, the "We will" statements are single efforts, such as special events or activities. In other cases, however, "We will" statements involve multiyear approaches to complex and systemic issues.

When we consider leading a school, it is important to note the relative importance of the many activities that occur in a school day. Value in leadership means defining what matters most so that all can begin to understand what the business of the school is. As we articulate the core values, the guiding and philosophical principles, all decisions can emerge from a shared belief. The synergistic effect is that we can begin putting our energy toward specific values, avoiding the ad hoc decisions characteristic of many schools. What the student, teacher, leader, and community see reflected in the activities of the school is a value-driven institution with a vision for where it is going, rather than an event-driven body. Just as with value in art, core values speak to all other elements of leadership. When done well, core values become the guiding principles for all decisions.

NIGHT DANCE AUTUMN LADIES, 2000

Acrylic, charcoal, India ink on paper, 50 × 40 in.
Collection of Cincinnati Art Museum, OH
Gift of Dr. and Mrs. William Tsiaras

Element No. 3

Shape: Two-dimensional area.

The Artist's View

A shape is a two-dimensional area that is defined in some certain way. By
drawing an outline of a circle on a piece of paper, one creates a shape. By

painting a solid red square, one also creates a shape. Shapes may be either free-form or geometric. Free-form shapes are uneven and irregular, and they usually induce a pleasant and soothing feeling. Geometric shapes, on the other hand, are stiff and uniform, and they generally suggest organization and management, with little or no emotion. Shape tends to appeal more to viewers' minds than to their emotions.

Shape as a Case Study

It is a typical first week of school for the principal at Round About Elementary. The principal has no idea how typical it is, because it is her first year in the position. On Monday, the school buses were late. One bus arrived 45 minutes after the start of school. On Tuesday, the cafeteria workers informed her that the ovens were not working and that there would be no lunch that day. On Wednesday, she is met at the door by Ms. Rookie, the new teacher, who has lost her keys to the classroom and proceeds to inform the principal: "I simply cannot work with Ms. Parapro. She is no help at all. I need you to find me someone else." Also, the principal hears from the central office that the students will be eating sack lunches all week, as the repair in the kitchen is going to take some time. Wednesday afternoon she is about to leave for the day when a student shows up at her door. She had ridden the bus home, found no one there, and walked back to school to find help. Thursday the finance director arrives to go over the revised budget and reminds the principal that there is no money for staff development this year. Friday morning there is an IEP meeting, and the Director of Special Education is at a conference. The superintendent wants to go over her expectations for the coming year today. Also, the reading material has yet to arrive from the publisher, and the third-grade teachers want to know what to do for next week's instruction. Shortly after lunch, the principal receives a message from a local Evangelical Congregation of the United States; they need to use the facility over the weekend for church services.

Welcome to the world of management of school programs. A leader's ability to come to terms with the competing demands of school necessarily and directly affects the school's capacity to offer a safe, orderly learning environment.

A Leadership Perspective

Schools have a shape, a smell, a look, a feel. As we imagine our elementary school days, we create physical images that capture our learning experiences. Similarly, as we walk into the elementary school just before lunch to smell the bread cooking in the dining hall, we are taken back to some of our favorite, or maybe not so favorite, memories of schooling.

Whatever the quality of those memories, they are certainly vivid. We watch the big yellow school bus traveling down the road and wonder about the children in that lovely "monster" of a vehicle. These images are not about instruction. They are about the other things that inform our memories and have deeply affected our lives. And even though they are not instruction, they are important to the successful school. They are the shape of schooling.

Management is the shape of schools. We manage budgets, discipline, community relations, and personnel. These are not the things that should be our focus in schools, but they are exactly the matters with which we must deal so that we might teach children. The effectiveness with which a leader can handle aspects of time management, scheduling, random but daily details, personnel management, parent conferencing, and community relations will determine the level of success of the students at that school.

Of the management details, supervision of personnel is the most rewarding, demanding, and exhausting. Successful leaders find ways to be instructional leaders, by offering supervision, staff development, remediation, and when necessary, termination. But during the whole process of management, leaders struggle to balance being feeling and supportive with being clinical and direct with personnel. Both sets of skills are necessary, but it is the rare leader who can do them both well. Effective leaders understand how to shape the modes of management to support the business of student learning.

A FENCE FOR JOSEPH, 1988

From the series "Urban Memoirs"
Acrylic on paper, 22 × 30 in.
Collection of Duncan and Diana Johnson, Providence, RI

Element No. 4

Form: Three-dimensional structure or shape; geometric or free-form.

The Artist's View

Forms are shapes that are three-dimensional, either geometric or free-form. In two-dimensional works of art—that is, artworks that hang on a wall—artists use value on a shape to create a form. In other words, when artists add value to the shape of a circle, the shape becomes a sphere and takes on the illusion of a something that is three-dimensional, a form. Today artists refer to lights and darks of a work of art as "modeling" or "shading." Very dark areas of forms tend to recede into the artwork, whereas very light areas appear closest to the viewer. In three-dimensional art, such as sculpture, all shapes are forms, because they take up space in three dimensions. True forms occupy height, width, and depth in space.

Form as a Case Study

The parents of Marjorie Settle come to you, the middle school principal, to complain that Marjorie has received a "zero" for a report in her social studies class. Her sixth-grade teacher had given the following directions regarding the assignment: "Your topic must be decent, researchable, and approved by me. You must have at least four bibliographic references in your report. Obtain my approval for your topic before proceeding." Six weeks after receiving this assignment, Marjorie was given a big, fat goose-egg for her report on Jesus Christ. Marjorie had on at least five occasions attempted to obtain approval for her report from the teacher, but was denied each time. The teacher had denied Marjorie's topic for two reasons: concern that the topic would foster an Establishment Clause violation, and Marjorie's insistence that a single bibliographic reference, the Bible, was adequate for her research.

When we recognize the important role that perspective has for understanding a given situation, we also see the real importance that empathy has for successful leadership. Empathy is the capacity to understand and identify another person's feelings or difficulties. In the case study above, the principal clearly needs to support the teacher but also recognize the motivation and perspective of the student. As the principal communicates to the teacher the different levels of issues included in this potentially emotional decision, he can simultaneously communicate trust and commitment through the effective use of communication. In so doing, emotions can be addressed so that reason might prevail.

A Leadership Perspective

The difference in management and leadership is the movement from shape to form, from a two-dimensional perspective to a three-dimensional one. Leadership is often a matter of perspective. Effective leaders find ways to recognize different perspectives through active listening. Specifically, they can discern surface messages and distinguish them from the very important, but embedded, messages. What is the speaker saying? What is the speaker communicating? What is the speaker feeling? The answers are often wide-ranging.

Communication has as its prerequisite trust. Without a sense of trust between two people, both in terms of content and confidentiality, there is little hope of meaningful conversation. An obvious example might be that if teachers trust their colleagues to work with them and not reveal their teaching weaknesses to the general public, and certainly not to supervisors, they might be more inclined to share deficiencies with colleagues. In so doing, teachers might be able to find help toward improving pedagogical gaps. If, on the other hand, teachers do not have confidence that others are genuinely concerned about their professional development, they will certainly not engage in conversation with people about any professional areas of need. It is through active listening that principals can communicate the trust and genuine interest that might lead to collegial interaction and growth.

Fortunately, active listening is a skill that can be developed. Though many people might think they are good listeners, in fact few people without concentrated and frequent practice, and perhaps training, are effective listeners. It is only through intentional practice that one can develop into an effective listener. And the truly good listener recognizes that communication comes in verbal and nonverbal forms (see appendix E).

Effective leaders also recognize that through empathic writing, a sort of active listening through writing, the content of a message can begin to have depth, along with breadth. In other words, leaders see the message from the front, from the side, from the inside. In so doing, the effective leaders recognize the multidimensional dynamic, the three-dimensional reality that comes with effective communication.

UNTITLED, 2001

From the portfolio "Suite 16, AS220"
Suite of 16 prints
Lithograph, sheet size: 30 × 15 in.
Collection, AS220, Providence, Rhode Island

Element No. 5

Space: Area around, between, above, below, or within an object.

The Artist's View

All the area that exists around, between, above, below, and within an object is considered to be space. Forms and shapes are considered to be "positive" space; that which occupies the area in and around the form and shape is called "negative" space. Artists that utilize large negative spaces may express loneliness or freedom. Crowding together positive space reflects tension or togetherness. Positive and negative spaces depend upon each other, interacting to create meaning. Space in three dimensions is considered the area that is over, under, around, behind, and through. Sculpture, jewelry, architecture, weaving, and ceramics are three-dimensional art forms. They are artworks that take up real space.

Space as a Case Study

As a new teacher, Mr. Protégé has the benefit of working with Ms. Mentor. Mr. Protégé came highly recommended on the basis of his academic achievement. He is described as earnest, hardworking, and extremely conscientious. He dresses very neatly and is polite almost to a fault. He uses a question-and-answer method almost exclusively. Mr. Protégé says that the children (sixth-graders) have to learn the facts before they can interpret, and that he hopes that everyone will master the material in the lesson plan. He follows his lesson plan literally.

In a meeting with Ms. Mentor, Mr. Protégé appears with a notebook and asks at least twenty-five questions about methods. He carefully writes down the answers. In between his questions about methods he asks questions about certification and appears confused about what he is expected to do as a first-year teacher. He is very serious and rarely shows humor. In general, he exhibits little awareness of feelings.

Mr. Protégé is like many first-year teachers who feel overwhelmed by the seemingly unending demands that come their way. Allowing him to have space to grow but not allowing him to be alone is a difficult balance for school leadership. However, effective leadership understands the role of support and challenge in creating space for professional development, in order for young teachers to grow to higher levels of effectiveness.

A Leadership Perspective

When a teacher works alone, he often has fewer skills for problem solving than if he worked with an older or more experienced person—that is, a mentor. The mentor can help the teacher explore different, and often new, ways to solve problems through trial and error or through approximations of existing schema. For example, if new learning is conceptually close to what the new teacher already knows and understands, he can more readily internalize it. If, however, the new learning is significantly different from what is already known, then the teacher will likely encounter more difficulty. In this case, a mentor can assist the teacher in identifying new pathways of understanding. Mentoring can enhance the ability to internalize new and difficult material. The simultaneous effort of support and challenge on the part of a mentor offers a productive model for learning. For example, the mentor might support learning by first presenting material that the teacher already understands and then challenging him with information that is an extension of that understanding. Put more directly, a teacher learns best when learning is connected to existing understanding; teacher learning is social in nature.

Understanding the role of space can help leaders create learning places that are at once challenging and supporting. Teaching assignments and the pedagogy that come with them help create challenge. Leaders help teachers grow and stretch by challenging them to take on different subjects, different age groups of students, different roles. Additionally, leaders create positive moments as they encourage teachers to use a wide range of pedagogical techniques in order to reach more students. Left alone, teachers can feel stretched but not appreciated; these challenges can create negative working conditions. Effective leaders find a way to balance challenge with support. Much as space in art is constructed with positive and negative aspects, successful learning space is constructed with a balance of support and challenge. The appropriate balance might include new teaching methods but at the same time opportunities for team planning or for coaching. Through sustained, long-term, embedded coaching and support, leaders offer teachers a safe environment where risks are valued and mistakes are acknowledged as part of the growing process.

SPANISH GARDEN NO. IV, 1994–95

From the series "Spanish Gardens"
Acrylic on paper, 50 × 40 in.
Collection of David and Carol Bazarsky, Newport, RI

Element No. 6

Color: Property of objects coming from reflected light.

The Artist's View

Color is the most dynamic and exciting element of art. It is also the hardest element to describe. Color comes from reflected light. When light is reflected

from an object such as a red ball, the red ball absorbs all light waves except red. The red light waves reflect into our eyes and are interpreted by our brain as the color red. Often, we represent colors along a spectrum—primary (red, yellow, and blue), secondary (violet, green, and orange), and tertiary or intermediate (red orange, red violet, blue violet, blue green, yellow green, yellow orange). When these spectral colors are bent into a circle, we form a color wheel. White and black are not considered colors at all; black is the absence of color, and white is the combination of all colors.

Color as a Case Study

Mr. Collaboration, superintendent of the local school district, enjoys having teachers work together on systemwide projects. He believes that the more he involves people in decision making, the more likely they are to get along and help create positive learning environments for students. In selecting people for participation in the projects, Mr. Collaboration wonders if it might be best to put people together with similar personality types or to mix the styles within groups.

The curriculum committee, however, concerns Mr. Collaboration. The Assistant Superintendent for Instruction, who has been in the district for 31 years, leads this committee, and she clearly has a special reading program she wants the school board to adopt. Her leadership style tends to intimidate other members of her committee. Additionally, she is not likely to embrace differing perspectives, and there is gossip about that she can make life tough on teachers who disagree with her.

Mr. Collaboration has a special challenge before him: How can he encourage the assistant superintendent to be more open to others' ideas? How might he pressure her to change her leadership style without being guilty of what he is accusing her of doing to other teachers? In a broader sense, then, Mr. Collaboration wants a culture in his district of openness and collaboration, but some of his important leaders do not agree with his perspective.

A Leadership Perspective

As different colors contribute to the whole beauty of the art, people's different styles, different gifts support successful schools. One of the ways leaders can celebrate differences is first to acknowledge that diversity is valued. This diversity can be in terms of gender or ethnicity, of course. What might also be noted is that a diversity of ideas, or of teaching styles, or of perspective is important to the successful school as well. Successful leaders consider learning styles and personality types as they seek out teachers' help. Building a successful committee is as much about "who decides who decides" as it is about who will be in the group. In other words, successful leaders help bring together individuals with acknowledged differences so that a true exchange of ideas can begin. The negative approach might be leaders who select the "right" ones for committees knowing before the work begins what their conclusions will be. Where leadership is successful there are shared values and goals coupled with an appreciation for the different paths one might take to reach those goals.

SPANISH FLOWER, 1994–95

From the series "Spanish Gardens"
Acrylic on paper, 30 × 22 in.
Collection of Dr. and Mrs. William Tsiaras, Barrington, RI

Element No. 7

Texture: Feel or appearance of an object or surface.

The Artist's View

Texture is the art element that refers to how things feel or look as if they might feel. We perceive texture through touch and vision. One can use tactile sensitivity, using skin receptors to feel texture, but one can also experience visual texture, by looking at the illusion of a three-dimensional surface. Once again, the element of value comes to the forefront. Without the relative lightness and darkness of the surface arrangement, the illusion of a surface texture could not be seen. Texture is important to every art medium.

Texture as a Case Study

Over the last ten years, the ethnicity of Homogeneous School District has changed radically. Because of a booming labor market in the area, there has been an expansion of migrant and immigrant labor in the community. As a result, the school population has changed from a majority white district to a predominantly minority district. The white parents are expressing a growing concern over the educational experiences of their children in light of the district's attempt to address the special needs of students with limited English skills. As superintendent of the district, you see clearly that this is not the case. You imagine that what is probably happening is that the white community is using academic quality as a "code" for discomfort with different students. They want their children to remain in classes with other white students, segregated from the growing minority group.

Your challenge is to embrace the "newcomers" without alienating the "old guard." In what ways might the district bring the two groups together in a celebration of diversity and academic excellence?

A Leadership Perspective

Successful school leaders recognize that schools are a tapestry of people, interests, and communities. Weaving those very different, and very important, stakeholders is a delicate and intricate process. If that is done well, the school becomes a seamless fabric celebrating student achievement. Done poorly, the school begins to unravel into patches of angry parents, frustrated teachers, and misbehaving students. Successful leaders take the time to invite participation by all stakeholders. This invitation, then, would be offered to parents, community leaders, students, teachers, administrators, and support staffs. The more these constituencies are included, the more commitment there will be by all concerned and the less opportunity for subterfuge and negative energy. The notion that we are all in this together would elevate the commitment for all.

CONCLUSION ON THE ELEMENTS OF SCHOOL LEADERSHIP

The elements of art juxtaposed to leadership provide us with symbolic language for understanding what makes for successful school leadership. As might be perceived in viewing different art forms, some elements are more obvious or more significant in one instance than in another moment or place. Such is the case with the elements of school leadership. Line, value, shape, form, space, color, and texture all contribute to quality schooling. Given one school with a certain set of needs, we might find that shape is the leading element. At another school with very different needs, however, we might find that texture is a focus. In playing a piano or singing in harmony, there are individual notes, but it is the collective, simultaneous action that elicits a full, coherent, and complete effect. The successful school leader has all seven elements at her command, albeit at different levels. And because she understands the interrelated nature of the elements, she is able to orchestrate a successful learning and teaching experience for her students and teachers.

QUESTIONS FOR DISCUSSION

1. Given the seven elements listed in this chapter, which one(s) do you feel most comfortable with? Why?
2. Which element do you lack command of? What might be some specific strategies for developing that element?
3. Identify one element that you believe would be useful for many leaders and design a staff development program for your school where you could introduce and develop that element.
4. Reflect on current realities at your school setting and identify one problem as an area for growth. Develop an action plan that uses one or more of the elements to facilitate your school's effort to address that problem. In your action plan, remember to identify a specific goal, some potential obstacles, a timetable, and a method of assessment, for determining your level of success.
5. Select one of the case studies and apply the following "Art of Leadership Critique." Remember to describe what happened, analyze particular behaviors, find meaning, and evaluate the leadership.

Art of Leadership Critique
Topic/Issue at Hand:_____
Leader Name:_____
School/System Setting:_____
Date:_____

Step 1: Description
The goal is to describe objectively what you see; to delay judgment. List system, leader, date; describe setting and key players; identify central or core issue; identify elements of leadership that are present.
A description might include: _____

_____

_____

Step 2: Analysis
The goal is to describe behaviors of what you see. Describe how the elements listed in step 1 use the principles of leadership. Which

principles provide organization for the elements? List your emotional reaction to these factors. How does the leadership strategy make you feel? How does it make others feel?

The analysis might include: _____

_____

_____

Step 3: Interpretation

The goal is to find meaning in what you see. Does it work? Why? What do you think the leader is trying to do? What is the goal? What are the symbolic goals that emerge? What do they mean?

One interpretation might be: _____

_____

_____

Step 4: Judgment

The goal is to evaluate what you see. How could the leader have been more successful? Who benefits from the decisions? Who does not? What balance is there between what the leader says, what he does, and what he believes? What is the relationship between what the school values, believes, and does?

A possible judgment would include: _____

_____

_____

4

Using the Principles
to Describe Leadership

Principles of design are the rules that govern how artists organize the elements of art. Another way of imagining it is that the principles offer the cohesive force that helps prevent the elements from standing apart from each other. Principles are the organizing forces that extend meaning for combinations of elements. The principles of design are emphasis, rhythm, movement, balance, proportion, variety, and harmony/unity.

In terms of leadership, I imagine that the principles of design are the ways that leaders select and arrange the elements to create a school atmosphere focused on student learning and teacher development. Put another way, they are the organizing and philosophical guides to making decisions daily, weekly, and yearly. In a given setting, there might be several elements at work that are held together by one principle. Or, there might be several elements present and multiple principles at work simultaneously. Let us for the moment take each of the principles separately and begin to understand their power to organize and synergize elements.

ON THE LAKE FRONT, 1988

From the series "Urban Memoirs"
Acrylic on paper, 40 × 26 in.
Collection of Mr. and Mrs. William Vareika, Newport, RI

Principle No. 1

Emphasis: one part of a work is dominant over the other parts. The element noticed first is dominant; the elements noticed later are subordinate.

The Artist's View

When we talk about emphasis, we are recognizing a particular element that stands out in an artwork. For example, as we view an abstract painting, our first reaction might be one of confusion. Upon closer examination, however, we begin to notice certain colors or shapes that tend to dominate the painting. We also notice that other elements, such as line or shape, are present but are not as obvious. In this way the observer begins to conceptualize and organize the painting's meaning through the use of emphasis.

Emphasis as a Case Study

At Brookhaven Elementary School, the principal is interested in communicating an inclusive philosophy in his rapidly changing school zone. Over the past five years, children from as many as nine different countries have joined his school. These newcomers have added to an already fluid cultural setting where 12 distinct countries had already been represented.

The principal has utilized all seven elements of effective leadership but decided to pay special attention to texture as a dominant theme in the school. Surrounding the American flag at the entrance of the school are flags flying for each country represented by his children. Every hall has a different art theme. Different classes are responsible for developing a concept, painting it, and displaying it in identified areas throughout the school. Outside the school, in the back at the playground, all walls are awash with painted histories of countries. He likes to think of this area as graffiti with a purpose! Each month a cultural Olympics is held, where sports and pastimes from various countries are studied, practiced, and played. The dining hall offers theme weeks, when menus reveal cultural influences. Corresponding to the dining themes are dress code themes. Instead of falling into the struggle of enforcing a dress code, the principal imagines that the theme weeks might actually help create a positive and exciting environment in his school. And finally, during the summer with staff development funds, the principal calls in lead teachers from the various grades to organize the curriculum scope and sequence from kindergarten to grade five. The teachers develop themes around which reading, mathematics, science, social studies, art, music, and physical education can create units of study. For example, during Mexico week a visitor finds that students in all grades, in all subject areas, are studying their subjects with Mexico as the major theme. The basics are still the focus. Teachers and students still recognize that they need to do well on standardized tests. But amid the important work of schooling, the principal emphasizes the leadership element of texture as a way to celebrate the children that are his school.

A Leadership Perspective

For leadership emphasis is about identifying significant realities of the school and then deciding how best to build positively on those realities. These realities are not necessarily significant in a statistical sense, although they might very well be so; rather, they are significant in that they are easily noted by teaching staffs and visitors alike. The realities might come in the form of physical characteristics of the building or of the neighborhood. The realities could be a reflection of the demographic composition of the student body. Curricular programs or magnet programs might generate a perceptual reality of the school community. Or, the realities might be about sports, band participation, cheerleading, and the like.

The harsh reality of emphasis, however, is that there is an emphasis that emerges in the school whether the leadership embraces it or not. That emphasis might come from the rituals that communicate tradition and culture (e.g., pep rallies on Fridays). It might come from a misdirected editorial in the local newspaper or a harshly written television program. The perception might be that nothing good is going on at the school, because no one has taken the initiative to communicate the exciting and positive things that are happening. In the void of information, I am afraid that local community sometimes assumes the worst.

Given these possibilities, the prudent leader and teachers can decide to be victims of the emphasis that others create, or they can take it upon themselves to create an emphasis that captures what is most important at the school, what is valued, what matters most. Embracing the principle of emphasis, the school leadership can fashion a culture that has one of the elements of leadership as the dominant theme, with the other six playing supporting roles.

In the case study above, that is what the principal has done. He has decided to focus on emphasis as a defining principle for the year; he has then taken up the reality of his school's changing population and let texture be the dominant element; and he has allowed the other six elements to play important but supporting leadership roles for his school. Matters of texture are clearly driving decisions about curriculum, dress code, and lunch menus; at the same time color, form, line, shape, space, and value continue to be important, albeit subordinate, leadership attributes for the principal.

AUTUMN LUST, 1997–1998

Acrylic on canvas, 54 × 44 in.
Collection of Kimberly Kelly, Bedford Hills, NY

Principle No. 2

Rhythm: indicates movement by the repetition of elements. The five types are random, regular, alternating, flowing, and progressive.

The Artist's View

In architecture designers often utilize rhythm in constructing buildings, houses, bridges, landscapes, and the like. In some interpretations, the

rhythm provides the "heartbeat" of the work. It is the life-giving force or principle. Consider the Golden Gate Bridge in San Francisco. The precise vertical lines create a pattern or "beat" to the visual image. The swooping, plunging cables sustain the life of the vertical cables. In their predictable repetitions, each set of cables offers life-sustaining support to the others, and certainly to the travelers on the road. There is certainty and safety, a sense of permanence, in the use of rhythm.

Rhythm as a Case Study

At the middle school, Ms. Wake is an impressive teacher of students with special needs. In ways that so many others fail, she can take students with the most challenging behavior problems and make angels out of them. Well, at least for the fifty minutes she teaches them, they are angels. As the students arrive from their physical education class, Ms. Wake always has soft music playing in her room. The faint scent of recently burned candles hangs as lightly as early morning mist. The walls are painted with soft images of landscapes and cityscapes. Stars hang randomly across the ceiling. There are green plants and hanging baskets about her room. In the corner of the room there is a loft where students can climb for reading and thinking, or they can go underneath for puzzles. Ms. Wake has an old, white claw-foot tub filled with pillows where students can write in their journals or read storybooks. But most importantly to the students, Ms. Wake's classroom is a place where they are welcomed and embraced. Every day she stops what she is doing as they enter the class and calls each student by name. Her room is a sanctuary. It has a rhythm of its own. And there, students feel safe.

A Leadership Perspective

Each classroom has a rhythm that is in large part a creation of the teacher. Teachers communicate an important message from the first moment that a student walks into the classroom. That message might be positive or negative, but the message is there. During the first few moments the rhythm of the class becomes clear. When teachers and students are prepared, much can be accomplished. When, on the other hand, in the first minutes teachers and students are rushing about, calling the roll, sharpening pencils, or finding supplies, much is lost.

Making it through the first moments of class is important but not sufficient for a good lesson. During the course of the lesson one of the most frustrating things that can happen to disrupt the rhythm can be an intercom call. In a somewhat odd twist of fate, in many instances we have replaced the intercom with phones in the rooms and computers "beeping" the arrival of new e-mail. The implications for leadership are obvious.

If a principal subscribes to the notion that rhythm is important to successful schooling, an important responsibility arises to protect the sanctity of the classroom from interruptions. Schools are defined by what happens in classrooms. When those classrooms are orderly, neat, inviting, and protected, students receive a positive message. When, however, the rooms are not so orderly, neat, inviting, or protected, schools communicate to students that learning comes last.

As with emphasis, rhythm becomes a focus for both teachers and principal. All matters related to the school day have as the primary consideration the possible consequences on the rhythm of the classroom. Do we have an assembly? If yes, how do we address the loss of instructional time? Do we follow block scheduling, or do we use 45-minute classes? How does each choice affect the rhythm of the classroom? When will it be appropriate to use the intercom, and how do we manage e-mail? Leadership answers these questions from the perspective of rhythm. Although rhythm is the driving force behind many decisions, the school leadership continues to find ways to support the seven elements of effective leadership, especially as they support the rhythm of the classroom.

EARLY MORNING AUTUMN MIST, 1998–1999

Acrylic on canvas, 44 × 44 in.
Collection of Joseph S. Gallo, Providence, RI

Principle No. 3

Movement: deals with creating the illusion of action or physical change in position.

The Artist's View

The artist, through the use of line, shape, and color, generates a feeling of turning and moving. The observer might "feel" the wind blowing through a

tree as it moves back and forth. Additionally, the lines can lead our eyes from the left side of the painting to the right side, as if carried by the wind. Whereas one might think of a painting in terms of a quiet and still setting, the artist can produce the sensation of movement through the interaction of various elements of art.

Movement as a Case Study

At Monumental High School, the leadership team is considering implementing block scheduling for the next school year. The previous summer the assistant principal and two department chairs attended a staff development program that examined alternative scheduling options for large high schools. It is early in the year, and the team imagines that it ought to use the remaining six faculty meetings to introduce and develop the innovation.

At the next faculty meeting, the principal introduces the leadership team and has them explain block scheduling. In that explanation is some discussion about A/B blocking or half-year blocking, about teaching strategies, about learning possibilities. It all seems very exciting. The staff leaves the meeting abuzz with conversation about the innovation. The few weeks after the introduction of block scheduling, three "camps" of influence begin to emerge.

There are the excited advocates, who just cannot see why anyone would question such a clearly superior plan for scheduling. The assistant principal and the two department chairs lead them. At the middle perspective, where the principal sits, is a group of teachers who really do not care what the decision is, "just so someone will hurry up and let them know." The principal is interested in producing the least amount of conflict, wherever that leads. At the other extreme is the "it ain't broke and we don't need to fix it" group led by Ms. Polly Permanent and Mr. Tom Tenure, both longtime veterans at the school. They are certain that if they garner enough support from the "undecided vote" they can disrupt yet another innovation and their positions in the school culture will remain unchallenged.

In the next two faculty meetings the two most extreme camps maneuver, cajole, undercut each other. Allegiances and alliances are the order of the day. Out of three "camps" two sides of the issue emerge: either a teacher is for the assistant principal/block scheduling, or the teacher is for Mr. Tenure and the status quo. The principal announces that everyone has enough information and that at the next faculty meeting he would call for a vote on the issue of block scheduling.

A Leadership Perspective

During the staff development days prior to the starting of school, the staff adopted the seven principles as guiding themes for the high school. The staff defined movement as that principle that supports continuity of learning through the synchronized passage of students throughout the school day. The block scheduling option addressed several principles in a general way but seemed to speak to movement specifically. For the school, movement represented the physical characteristics of the school day that might support or impede student learning. The teachers at this high school found that having six or seven periods each day actually reduced learning time. The time students spent moving from class to class increased, thus taking away from an already crowded day. The time spent settling down and getting to work at each class period took away even more valuable instructional time. In some cases, teachers were left with 15 or 20 minutes of instructional time rather than 50 minutes. Block scheduling came to the staff as support for the principle of movement.

In light of these realities we might have concluded that the block scheduling, with its 90-minute lessons and only four schoolwide transitions during the day, was an obvious and logical choice. The resulting decisions, however, reflected more about internal politics and culture than about a shared commitment to the principle of movement. With the yes-or-no vote the principal inadvertently created two classes of teachers, winners and losers. At least as important, however, was the fact that the decision was made in the absence of the guiding principle of movement. What resulted was a negative school culture that communicated subtle, but disturbing, messages about how adults might interact with each other. When decisions can be made in the shadow of the guiding principles, the influence of individual agendas and personalities can disappear into the dark. In the absence of guiding principles, positive movement becomes more about "start and stall" than "start and grow."

UNTITLED, 2001

From the portfolio "Suite 16, AS220"
Suite of 16 prints
Lithograph, sheet size: 30 × 15 in.
Collection, AS220, Providence, Rhode Island

Principle No. 4

Balance: concerned with equalizing visual forces, or elements.

The Artist's View

By using balance artists can "frame" an object in a painting. An artist might also use the lack of balance to suggest confusion or frustration. The

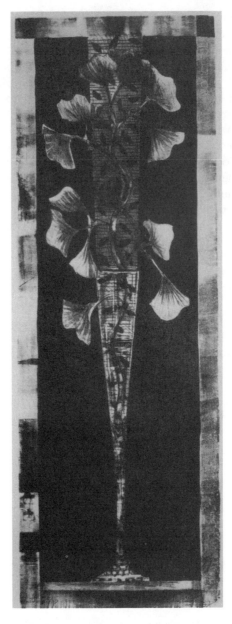

viewer might sense tension or maybe that something does not seem to be in order. Similarly, architects might find the use of symmetrical balance important to communicate a sense of stability, safety, and permanence. Or the architect might use patterns of material or structures to suggest balance or stability.

Balance as a Case Study

Dr. Lombardi has been principal for four years at one of the district's eleven elementary schools. He has just entered into his second three-year contract with the board of education. Dr. Lombardi came to the principal position after ten years as a teacher and football coach at the middle school.

Dr. Lombardi has always enjoyed working hard. He often put in 14-hour days as he tried to balance his work as coach and teacher. A surprise to him in this new job, however, is that at least four days each week he spends 14 hours at school, and weekends are often lost to school responsibilities. During the week, he arrives before 7:00 AM every day, because buses begin arriving at 7:05. After-school responsibilities vary from monitoring the After-School Program to attending open houses, athletic events, plays, musicals, fund-raisers, board meetings, and PTO meetings.

Lately, Dr. Lombardi has found he is quick to lose his temper, often frustrated with how little time he has at home, growing frustrated with parents and teachers, and tired all the time. He is a gifted leader, but he has begun to neglect his own health, both physical and emotional, in the interest of getting the work done at school. Maybe it is time for him to get out of education and enter into work that is more predictable and less draining.

The school district has instituted a mentoring program for its leadership team, and Dr. Lombardi has been asked to participate. In the process it has become clear to him that his job has taken over his life. If he wants to continue doing what he loves—working with students—then he must make some radical changes to his working style. If he does not take back his life, the schoolchildren will lose an important ally, his family life will continue to suffer, and his own health will deteriorate further.

A Leadership Perspective

Striking a balance between the demands of our personal and professional lives is a continuous struggle. It is clear, however, that when we fail to attend to the things that matter most to us, we begin to fail in all other areas as well. Leadership demands that we search for ways to support others, but it also calls on us to support ourselves.

Recognize that stress is a regular part of our lives. The difference between successful leaders and those who "burn out," however, is the way they handle or react to stress. Generally, the more time we spend doing things that we do not value, the greater the stress. In other words, if we want to work with children and our work has us doing everything *but* working with children, we have the makings of a highly stressful setting.

Effective leadership calls on us to decide what is valued in our personal and professional lives. Once we have articulated, and I suggest that means writing down, those values, we begin to understand the competing demands in our day. We make decisions based on how they affect our values. If an activity or responsibility challenges our guiding values, we will do one of three things: we will choose not to do the activity; we will recognize the activity is important but delegate it to someone else; or we will decide that the activity is so important that we will compromise in the short term our guiding principle. In this last choice, however, we will commit to "paying ourselves back" for sacrificing the principle. In other words, if we decide to stay late tonight to finish a report for the superintendent, we will schedule a time later in the week where we will leave early, or maybe have an ice cream or see a movie, as a "payback."

When we find that there are too many demands to remain loyal to our guiding principle of balance between our personal and professional lives, we might have to consider changing the nature of the work. This decision would not be an easy one, but the alternative of losing one's own health and personal life would be too high a price to pay for a job. The principle of balance challenges leaders to find grounding in our personal and professional lives, and in that grounding we will spend time on what matters most. In that way, we begin to attend to our family, our schoolchildren, and ourselves. And that is what matters most.

WAITING, PORTRAIT OF JACKIE ROBINSON, 1999

From the portfolio "Out at Home: Negro Baseball League, Volume I"
Lithograph, 30 × 22 in.
Collection of the Albright-Knox Gallery, Buffalo, NY

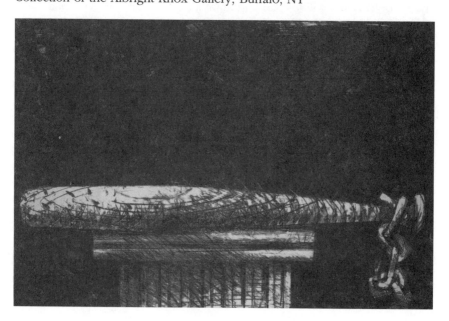

Principle No. 5

Proportion: concerned with the size relationships of one part or another.

The Artist's View

Artists recognize that people come in many shapes and sizes but that they generally have the same proportions. Often sculptors capitalize on this notion by placing certain portions of the body out of proportion to what one might normally expect. Take Michelangelo's *David* as an example. The sculpture is very tall, with head and hands slightly out of proportion to the rest of the body. Although several interpretations might account for this reality, one might conclude that Michelangelo wanted to emphasize the intelligence (e.g., head) and the strength (e.g., hands) as important parts of his message to the viewer. In so doing, the artist has used proportion as a tool of expression.

Proportion as a Case Study

The middle school is grappling with reduced funds for the coming year. As a result of a drop in tax revenues in the community, the district did not receive the funds it had anticipated for the approved budget. After much discussion in public meetings, the board of education called for a 3 percent decrease in the next year's budget. The superintendent has notified the middle school principal of the reduction in the operating budget, and now the principal, in the spirit of site-based management, must decide how to adjust.

The middle school prides itself on a wide range of curriculum offerings. In addition to the prescribed courses of study in English, mathematics, social studies, and science, the school boasts offerings in technology, foreign languages, physical education, art, music, home economics, and drama. This variety of offerings has been a luxury that became possible over the years when the funding was high and the economy solid. Now, things have to change.

One solution that is easy to imagine but painful to implement is to eliminate two of the extra offerings completely (e.g., foreign languages and drama). This choice is painful in part because it eliminates two full-time teachers. Although it is legal, it is rarely easy to release teachers in response to funding losses. Reducing the two programs also reduces opportunities for the increasingly diverse students to interact.

The principal and teachers are unwilling to eliminate the extra offerings. The state department guidelines, however, prevent any reduction in the core academic programs. Given that each of the programs is important to the students and staff, the leadership team sets out to look at the relative costs of each program compared to the total cost of operating the program. Because of the growing diversity in the student population, the leadership team decides to emphasize one of the foreign languages along with art, reducing them less than the other courses. Foreign languages and art are important to the staff and to the teachers; keeping them as priorities helps sustain the spirit and culture of the institution. Therefore, those two extra offerings remain important in proportion to time and money spent. In the end, the school has met the financial challenge by remembering the role that proportion can play in helping to make decisions that affect all. What was most important received a proportionate commitment in the budget.

A Leadership Perspective

Addressing competing demands quickly requires leadership to decide what matters most and what falls down the priority list. It becomes an exercise in proportionality. The things that are the most critical—highest in priority—begin to take a larger proportion of leadership's energy and time. Often, however, we find leaders spending the most time with the things that matter the least, resulting in a leader who is very frustrated, unfulfilled, and tired.

Proportion for leadership requires that we do two things. First, we identify all the demands on our lives, both personal and professional. That list should include everything that comes to us, from the simplest to the most complicated. Reviewing that list, we decide which of the items take up the most time and which ones take up the least. In so doing, we can begin to recognize how we spend our days.

Second, we take the list developed above and decide which things matter most to us and which matter the least. Finally, we compare the proportion of time we spend on the things we value most versus the amount of time we commit to the things we value least. The results of the comparison reveal that we spend the greatest amount of time on the things that are least important. And we wonder why we are tired all the time and often frustrated!

Successful leadership recognizes that when we are clear about what matters most and commit to spending a proportionate amount of time and energy in that endeavor, we will be more effective leaders, drawing strength and energy from that balance.

FIVE FIGURES, 1984

From the series "Strange Fruit"
Charcoal and ink wash on paper, 60 × 40 in.
Collection of the artist

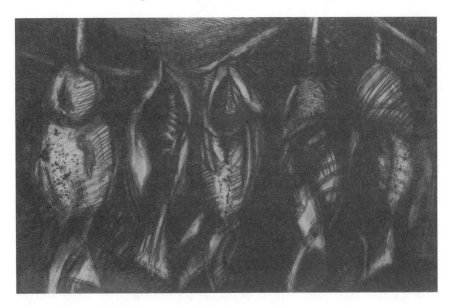

Principle No. 6

Variety: concerned with difference or contrast.

The Artist's View

Although a painting can represent a single moment in time, almost a snap-shot, the artist may use variety to create many stories at once. For example, the artist might position individuals in interesting ways so as to suggest "side" conversations amid the larger story. The contrast of individuals, in terms of both shape and color, can capture moments that are at once per-plexing and emotional.

Variety as a Case Study

The district recently adopted an assessment instrument for its teachers. Teachers who are in the first, second, or third year of experience are evalu-ated four times during the school year. Teachers who have more than three years' experience receive evaluations once a year. Additionally, however, the experienced teachers conduct observations of their younger colleagues. By following this type of peer evaluation, the district hopes to capitalize on the talents of the many experienced teachers. Also, the district encourages its teachers to collaborate and share effective teaching strategies. The goal of the assessment program is to encourage creative teaching strategies that share a common goal of student achievement.

At each faculty meeting, pairs of teachers present successes, challenges, and learning they have garnered by working together. The principal has posted a teaching bulletin board where the stories from the year are collected. By year's end all teaching pairs will have had the opportunity to share their experiences, and the evidence of the variety of teaching strategies will be displayed proudly. The excitement that comes with creative and exploratory energy is growing. Morale is high.

For the most part the program has worked well. Problems are beginning to emerge, however, with certain teachers who are evaluating practice based on their own preferences rather than on objective criteria, such as when students achieve lesson outcomes. For example, at last month's faculty meeting Mr. Pierson stated that group work is the best strategy for supporting student learning. "Everyone ought to be using cooperative groups!" he proclaims loudly. His less experienced colleague, Ms. Hide, chooses lecture, question and answer, and practice work as the best way to help students to learn. She is in her first years of teaching and when asked about group work, she responded, "Group work? I am just trying to survive what I am doing now. I cannot even imagine doing group work with these three preparations I have. Maybe next year I will give it a try." What we have is a classic notion of variety: contrast and difference!

So the principal has two very different teaching strategies presented at the faculty meeting. Both Mr. Pierson and Ms. Hide have successfully completed their evaluations. Student performance for both has been high, as well. The challenge for the principal is to find a way to celebrate the variety of teaching strategies that support high standards without standardizing teaching practice and discouraging creativity.

A Leadership Perspective

One the balancing acts of leadership is promoting standards while encouraging variety. Although at first glance one might recognize that standards are about levels of competence, it is in the misapplication of standards that problems begin to arise. Sound leadership comes to recognize that we can encourage variety in pedagogy without compromising achievement. Some leadership philosophies, however, mistakenly associate standardization of programs of instruction, ones that are "teacher proof," with high standards for performance.

We begin searching for the "silver bullet," the magic teaching strategy that when applied to all students by all teachers will improve all performance. If students do not improve their scores, the problem lies in the teacher's application of the unit, not anywhere else. As instructional leaders we know that this type of thinking is painfully wrong. It is painful for the teachers and for the students.

Most everything we know about learning reminds us that success in schooling is about connecting to different students by different means. To orchestrate such connectedness requires teachers who understand the variety of needs that students bring to the classroom. It also requires leadership that comprehends the need for autonomy characteristic of successful teachers.

HIGH NOON LOLITA, 1992–1993

Acrylic on canvas, 49 × 39 in.
Collection of Dr. and Mrs. Joseph Chazan, Providence, RI

Principle No. 7

Unity/Harmony: Unity is the quality of wholeness or oneness that is achieved through simplicity, repetition, proximity, and continuation. Harmony creates unity by stressing similarities of separate but related parts.

The Artist's View

What is it about a work of art that makes it feel like it goes together? In what ways do the parts seem to fit? Sometimes it is the sheer act of repeating an element throughout the work that suggests unity. At other times, the artist builds conceptual bridges between separate parts of the work, emphasizing their similarities. Consider music as an example of harmony. When separate but related notes are struck, a harmonizing effect emerges. The notes are separate, but the combined sound builds a unity within the work. Visually, a design artist might create wholeness in a clothing line by repeating patterns or colors in a variety of ensembles. Conversely, maybe the lack of decorative designs and multiple colors creates a sense of simplicity that unifies a line of clothing. The visual artist might complete a painting of five individuals in a street scene. They have nothing in common, but by being in the same place at the same time, looking at the same child eating an ice cream, they become joined. They are metaphorically in touch with each other. The artwork, thus, achieves a type of unity or harmony.

Unity/Harmony as a Case Study

It is the first day of school, and the principal is rushing to meet the children coming off the bus. The teachers are busy with last-minute classroom preparations. The first big yellow bus arrives and the children step off into their new world. The shoes are new, the clothes are clean, the backpacks display all the latest toys and cartoon characters. The principal has a call from the

central office to meet with a board member. There seems to be a personnel matter with which he must deal. "How can they expect me to be in both places?" he laments. He rushes back to his office, gets his coat, and heads to his car, near to where the buses are unloading their delicate charges. He backs up and heads out, but happening to look back at the school, he notices a child standing at the side of the building, tears rolling down her cheeks. He turns around in the middle of the street and returns to the parking spot.

As he approaches the child he asks, "What is wrong?" The child just shuffles and looks down. He bends to a knee, looks into her eyes, and asks, "How can I help you?" The child answers, "I cannot go into school. My father said that since I was old enough to be in school, I was old enough to tie my own shoe. And if I did not, then the other children would make fun of me." The principal, ignoring a second phone call from the central office, reaches down and ties her shoes, takes her by the hand, and walks her to her new room. The principal hands the child over to the teacher and says to the child, "Anytime you want help tying your shoes, you come and get me. Together we are going to have a very good year." The phone rings again; the principal starts to answer but instead turns it off and returns to bus duty.

A Leadership Perspective

Successful leadership is in many ways a function of our ability to be present in the moment. On a practical level this notion is about reflection on personal and professional experiences. As we rush to school to do the business of educating children, we can forget about the human element of our school world. In the past week, how many times have we paid attention—I mean really paid attention—to a friend, a colleague, or a child? An equally important question, and some folks might say a more important one, is how many times we have paid attention to our own needs and emotions. It is virtually impossible to be present with another person when we are not present with ourselves. For example, when a teacher comes to me with a problem from home and I am too busy thinking about the next chore or the approaching board meeting, I do him no good as a concerned and authentic colleague. I would do him a favor by saying, "Sorry, but I have too much to do to sit and listen to this." It might be a painful statement, but at least it would be a true one.

But no one would recommend responding to a colleague in this manner. The alternative, therefore, would be to make time for reflection so that we regain our energy, our perspective. The beneficiaries would be our friends, our children, and ourselves. Once we begin to create a harmony or unity within our own being, we become more useful as leaders and as caring human beings. And as we rush down the hall to have our next meeting, we will find time to stop and tie the shoes of a first-grader who awaits an uncertain home life.

CONCLUSION ON THE PRINCIPLES OF LEADERSHIP

The seven principles offer us organizing themes for understanding leadership in today's schools. Often, they can help us organize the elements of leadership. In each of the examples, we can find ways to organize our often-fractured efforts to support children in our schools. No one principle offers the best answer. But all principles, either together or alone, may offer us opportunities for doing what we know is best for students and their learning.

QUESTIONS FOR DISCUSSION

1. Given the seven principles listed in this chapter, which one(s) do you feel most comfortable with? Why?
2. Which principle do you lack command of? What might be some specific strategies for developing that principle?
3. Identify one principle that you believe would be useful for many leaders and design a staff development program for your school in which you could introduce and develop that principle.
4. Reflect on current realities at your school setting and identify one problem as an area for growth. Develop an action plan that uses one or more of the principles to facilitate your school's effort to address that problem. In your action plan, remember to identify a specific goal, some potential obstacles, a timetable, and an assessment for determining your level of success.
5. Which principle holds the greatest promise for you personally and professionally? How can you develop that principle more fully? How can you monitor your own growth?
6. Select one of the case studies and apply the following "Art of Leadership Critique." Remember to describe what happened, analyze particular behaviors, find meaning, and evaluate the leadership.

Art of Leadership Critique
Topic/Issue at Hand:_____
Leader Name:_____
School/System Setting:_____
Date:_____

Step 1: Description
The goal is to describe objectively what you see; to delay judgment. List system, leader, date; describe setting and key players; identify central or core issue; identify elements of leadership that are present.
A description might include: _____

_____

_____

Step 2: Analysis
The goal is to describe behaviors of what you see. Describe how the elements listed in step 1 use the principles of leadership. Which principles provide organization for the elements? List your emotional reaction to these factors. How does the leadership strategy make you feel? How does it make others feel?
The analysis might include: _____

_____

_____

Step 3: Interpretation
The goal is to find meaning in what you see. Does it work? Why? What do you think the leader is trying to do? What is the goal? What are the symbolic goals that emerge? What do they mean?
One interpretation might be: _____

_____

_____

Step 4: Judgment
The goal is to evaluate what you see. How could the leader have been more successful? Who benefits from the decisions? Who does not? What balance is there between what the leader says, what he does, and what he believes? What is the relationship between what the school values, believes, and does?
A possible judgment would include: _____

_____

_____

5

Elements, Principles, and Leadership: A Summary

Growing up in the north Georgia mountains, I was frequently perplexed with the notion of being able to see the forest for the trees. What did that mean, exactly? Why was it important to separate the trees from the forest? It did not make much sense to me as a child why we needed to make a distinction. All I needed was to climb trees, and that necessarily took me into the woods. Enough said! Well, it would seem that I have come full circle to my "roots" in wrestling with the elements of art and the principles of design. But in many ways, the forest-and-trees metaphor is exactly what I have brought to the front again by discussing the elements (trees) and the principles (forest) and their bearing on leadership. Allow me to explain.

As I have traveled around this country I have continually marveled at the different and exquisite landscapes. From airplane windows I have seen the patterns and colors of Kansas, the mountains of Colorado, the pines in Georgia, the coast of Maine, the great redwoods of California, the deserts of Arizona, the waters of Florida, and the endless terrain of Texas. From 30,000 feet I was able to get a real sense of the themes of the land below.

Upon landing in these places, I saw the specific attributes of the local terrain that had yielded the impressions from so high above. The mountains outside of Denver seemed to touch the city, but as I traveled to the Rocky Mountain State Park, the mountains continued to step back as if they resisted my arrival. The mountains became severe, extreme; from above they had appeared tall but not nearly so rugged. In California, I drove to Meir Woods and walked among the giant trees that from above created a smooth carpet of green. "This certainly must be how a flea feels in shag carpet," I marveled. The Georgia pines seemed so simple and consistent, but in the middle of them I found myself blinded by their complex maze. And how could I possibly get lost in a simple cornfield in the Midwest? The better question became, "How would I ever escape the unyielding grasp of the cornfield?"

The view from 30,000 feet is in part the way I conceptualize the principles of leadership. The very different perspectives I collected after landing represent my view of elements of leadership. Both views are necessary for a full understanding, but neither view is complete without the other. Some schools might have all six elements throughout the hallways, departments, classrooms, and administrative offices. For example, a social studies department chair gathers her staff to discuss her leadership style. She says to her group:

> Although we have no control over the Course of Study approved by the State Board of Education, I do think we have wide latitude in our various approaches to teaching. As we work together this year you will see in my approach to leading the department several of the elements of leadership. In lessons plans, I am more about shape. I like the details and delineation in your planning for student learning. In department meetings, I work from the basic assumption that I want to hear from each member stories about challenges and victories. The element of form helps me remember the core purpose of the meeting so that I can continue to see you and your work from all sides and perspectives. Throughout the year, you will note all the elements of leadership in my choices and in my work with you and by doing so, I hope to support the wide range of leadership strategies for myself and for you so that we can respond the diverse challenges that await us each day children arrive.

Other schools or groups within the school might be recognized by a very distinct set of one or two elements of leadership. For example, the math department head, just down the hall from the social studies department mentioned above, characterizes his leadership preference as an element of line. He works diligently in letting his colleagues know who is responsible for various responsibilities. He provides a detailed outline of the year, with special events highlighted. Also, different members of his department know which events they are primarily responsible for and what the expectations are for leading the event. Additionally, our math department head states:

> I want to honor how each of you manages your math classes. In saying this, I welcome different perspectives and ideas. I do expect, however, that we all provide for our students very clear ideas about classroom management. As a part of the leadership for me and for the leadership you model for your students, we will embrace the element of line as a reminder to be clear about our expectations. Students in all of our classes will see consistent rules for being prepared with the proper materials, for beginning class with an appropriate advanced organizer, for participating in class discussions, and for completing homework. We will likely have wide-ranging classroom activities, assignment types, and teaching styles, but within that range students will draw comfort in the predictable notions of expectations among all math teachers.

Similarly, some school leaders might focus on one principle as a philosophical and guiding light. Principles of design for leadership give us focus and perspective without making our view narrow or myopic. During preplanning, one school principal conducts a discussion of proportion at the first gathering of the teachers. According to him:

> At our school, we will let the principle of proportion guide us through our five-year plan, our yearly goals, and our daily decisions. We will make decisions regarding our expenditures of time, money, and staff based on our notions of what is important and on what matters most to student learning. And because proportion is concerned with the size relationships of one part to another we will reflect on our practice to make certain that we do not get out of proportion. We know that schools across the country have many common characteristics, but the difference between them is often a function of proportion. Our neighboring school has mistakenly allowed the athletics program to become disproportionate, both in terms of time and money, to the goal of student learning. That leadership has lost its sense of proportion. When we gather as a staff to discuss textbooks, testing schedules, pep rallies, PTO meetings, and the like, we will examine those decisions in light of how they support our long-term, annual, and daily goals. In so doing, we will come to school each day; we will not forget why we are here.

Other schools might find different principles helpful to one grade level, and another principle important to a different grade level or different subject areas. At the local middle school, the principal has worked throughout the summer with the leadership teams at the sixth-, seventh-, and eighth-grade levels toward deciding what each grade level's principle of design for leadership will be. It has become clear that what the sixth grade sees as its principle and what the eighth grade sees are very different. The sixth grade has committed to the principle of rhythm, particularly in terms of the use of block scheduling. At the sixth-grade meeting, the lead teacher states:

> When our children arrive they are entering a very new world as compared to their fifth-grade worlds. There is so much that is new and so little that is familiar. We will do our students a great service if within our teams of sixth grades we can allow rhythm to be our guiding principle. Remembering that rhythm speaks to movement by repetition, we can then help our students feel safe through the repetition of our schedules, our expectations, our teaching, and our classroom management. I am not interested in our doing the same thing every day, at every hour, for we would certainly deplete our students and ourselves of any excitement and energy. But, I am interested in building a rhythm that communicates predictability, and in so doing our students and teachers can feel safe to take risks without making our school a place that is both random and unpredictable.

In the eighth grade, the teachers have committed to a principle of harmony/unity. At the end of the year, teachers asked their seventh-graders to write a letter to the principal in which they could "wish for" anything at the school to help them during the eighth grade. Reading what their students had written, the principal and teachers were startled to recognize that their students had lost their ability to talk with each other and with teachers. The students spent so much time talking about differences that they lost their sense of what made them similar. The eighth-grade team leader states:

> Our students do not know how to talk to each other, and that is a problem. Our students do not know how to talk to us, and that, too, is a problem. But a greater problem is that neither our students nor we as teachers know how to listen to each other. The journals of the seventh graders again and again communicate that no one is listening. And then we wonder why there is so much strife and frustration with our eighth-graders. This year, we will embrace the opportunity to listen to each other and to our students. We will also help our students learn to listen to each other. Whether at lunch, at play, or at work, we will be an eighth grade guided by the principle of unity/harmony. In so doing, we will recognize our different needs and expectations, but more importantly we will begin to see our similarities and what we have in common.

At the one middle school, more than one principle of design for leadership was at work. At the very least, the principal subscribed to the principle of variety in his management of the school. He was concerned with helping the staff recognize difference and contrast versus trying to make them all be the same. So, in effect, we have a school with at least three principles of design for leadership at work simultaneously. What is notable is that principles do not compete with each other. They all provide a type of unifying guidance amid competing and potentially disruptive energies.

Principles of design for leadership offer us guiding and philosophical themes. Within the organizing assumptions of the principles, we find that the elements of art for leadership give us specific, discrete, and concrete ways to do and say what it is we value most.

QUESTIONS FOR DISCUSSION

1. Define one element of art and offer one example of how it might be used in an artwork.
2. Define one principle of design and offer one example of how it might be used in a work of art.
3. How are elements of art and principles of design different? How are they similar?
4. How can understanding elements of art help you become a better leader?
5. How might an understanding of the principles of design help you be an effective leader?

6. Identify an area of concern or need at your school. Choose one principle of design that might offer you an organizing theme for addressing that need. After selecting a principle, discuss how the elements will be used within that theme. (Remember, your elements can take on different forms and different strengths depending on how you develop your principle of design.)

6

Supervision as an Art Form: A Conceptual Basis

Let me make this point clear at the outset: I draw a sharp distinction between administration, evaluation, and supervision. For purposes of this book, administration is everything that school leadership does except instructional supervision. More specifically, school leaders have responsibilities that come to them through assignments that are either de jure (i.e., job descriptions) or de facto (i.e., customs or traditions) in nature. Some examples of de jure responsibilities are budget administration, bus duties, scheduling, parent and community conferences, lunchroom supervision, and extracurricular supervision. De facto responsibilities might include such activities as meeting parents at the dropoff line in the morning, attending town council meetings, or supporting student achievements at recognitions and banquets. These functions are critically important to ensuring a safe, orderly learning environment, but they are not supervision. Evaluation is that activity that involves assessment of teachers and staff for the purposes of continued employment, promotion, or termination. Again, these are essential responsibilities, but they are not a function of supervision as I see it. Thus I am left with the challenge of defining what supervision is. I draw comfort, in a distorted sort of way, from the fact that my struggle to define supervision adequately is a labor shared with many scholars. And this brings me to my second point: Definitions of supervision over the past fifty years have varied widely.

Given then that I know what supervision *is not*, let me share some ideas about what supervision *might be*. In this chapter I will attempt to establish a conceptual basis for supervision as an art form. In making such a case I do not necessarily intend to challenge the research-based, well articulated forms or versions of supervision, such as clinical, scientific, or developmental, for example. Rather, I am offering a perspective that attempts to invigorate and extend the conversation about what supervision can become. In other words, what we are doing in supervision is often done well, but there is more that we can do to support student achievement and teacher growth. I have come to believe in my years of supervisory practice that much of the supervision of teachers and leaders is indeed scientific, rational, and measurable. A quick review of virtually any state assessment instrument can reflect this belief (see the Alabama PEPE program, Georgia GTEP, or the South Carolina ADEPT for examples in the southeast). But I have also come to recognize that there is often an equal amount, quantitatively and qualitatively, of nonscientific, nonrational, nonmeasurable attributes of teaching. If our supervisory mode of operation is limited to only one or two strategies or methodologies, we risk missing the big picture of what is really happening in the classroom. I suggest that there is a fuller conception of supervision that recognizes and embraces what Pajak (2003) notes as the diversity of teaching and learning styles in today's schools. A brief discussion of various definitions or views of supervision followed by a framing of supervision as an art form will help develop these notions.

DEFINITIONS

School leadership has viewed supervision through the lens of social and historical context. During a time when teachers were viewed with suspicion, such as around 1900, supervision was investigation and interrogation. When, however, supervisors saw teachers as professionals, such as the 1970s and 1980s, supervision became more collaborative and collegial (Bolin, 1987; Glanz, 1998). Glanz noted seven models or definitions of supervision:

- Supervision as Inspection: Surprise visits to identify and remove incompetent teacher, not help them (p. 49).
- Supervision as Social Efficiency: "Scientific and bureaucratic methods of supervision aimed not at professionalizing but at finding a legitimate and secure niche for control-oriented supervision within the school bureaucracy" (p. 53).
- Supervision as Democratic Process: A focus on a more humane, moral, professional process for helping teachers; democracy vs. monarchical rule (p. 55).
- Supervision as Scientific Process: A move away from rating schemes to objective and scientific methodologies, moving supervision to a professional status (p. 57).
- Supervision as Leadership: "Provide leadership in five ways: developing mutually acceptable goals, extending cooperative and democratic methods of supervision, improving classroom instruction, promoting

research into educational problems, and promoting professional leadership" (p. 63).

- Supervision as Clinical Process: "Teaching can be improved by a prescribed, formal process of collaboration between teacher and supervisor. [Clinical supervision] eschewed any engagements with teachers that even remotely resembled inspectional, faultfinding supervision" (p. 63).
- Supervision as Developmental Process: Value placed on the notion of instructional leadership and instructional leader; value on collegiality (p. 63).

In each of the models we find an emerging and developing, albeit often disjointed and nonlinear, definition of supervision. The history of supervision moved from a definition of supervision, in its earliest manifestation as a function of finding and eliminating incompetent teachers by means of surprise visits, to the more recent definition of supervision as planned visits and collaborative planning for mutual or bidirectional improvement. But even as authors and researchers pushed this development, Glanz (1998) lamented: "Supervision as practiced in schools remained inspectional at worst and eclectic at best" (p. 63). In essence, then, we see that the articulation of what supervision is has taken on different definitions but its actual implementation has resisted moving away from the belief that supervision is in fact little more than inspection.

Eye and Netzer (1965) offer one explanation for such a variety of definitions. There are "so many different statements [because] each author develops one for the purpose of giving his own presentation a focal point that will lead to consistency and completeness of treatment" (p. 12). Harris (1998) suggests that among the diversity of definitions (e.g., supervision as craft, as science, as development, as evaluation) there are "many consistencies." Some of these are contained in definitions of supervision focused on:

- Teaching and learning
- Responding to changing external realities
- Providing support, assistance, and feedback to teachers
- Recognizing teaching as the primary vehicle for facilitating school learning
- Promoting new, improved innovative practices (p. 2).

More recently, supervision scholars (Pajak, 2000, 2003; Glickman, 2002; Glickman, Gordon, & Ross-Gordon, 2004; Sergiovanni & Starratt, 2002) have continued to wrestle with what supervision is and what it is not. These scholars do seem to agree with the fundamental assumption that supervision, when done well, can be characterized as developmental, clinical, collegial, or ethical. Reminding us of the continuing variety and sometimes ambiguity in defining supervision, Pajak's (2003) work presents four families of clinical supervision and their spokespersons:

- Original clinical models (Goldhammer; Cogan)
- Artistic/humanistic models (Eisner; Blumberg; and Barone)
- Technical/didactic models (Acheson & Gall; and Hunter)
- Developmental/reflective models (Glickman; Costa and Garmston; Zeichner and Liston; Garman; Smyth; and Waite). (p. 8)

Professional organizations dedicated to the support and refinement of instructional supervision have at times struggled with an adequate definition for the supervisory practice. One such group, the Council of Professors of Instructional Supervision (COPIS), emerged from the Association for Supervision and Curriculum Development (ASCD) in the 1970s. This group of scholars was concerned that the research focus for supervision was being lost in the diverse topics of ASCD. The COPIS organization began meeting in conjunction with national ASCD conferences in order to share current research, debate issues of supervision, and compile and publish articles related to supervisory theory and practice. This said, COPIS continues to wrestle with the best definition of what supervision is and most recently has undertaken an initiative to establish a set of standards for supervisory practice. Part of the benefit of a collection of standards may lie in a more cohesive understanding of what supervision is, not only with the COPIS organization but also with other school organizations and leaders who are commissioned to supervise but may not know precisely what that directive actually includes. In many ways, however, I find energy in the continued process of defining supervisory practice, for the effort clearly recognizes the complexities and subtleties embedded in helping teachers support student learning.

SUPERVISION AS ART FORM

In the foreword of this book I introduced the term "Arts-Based Research," and in chapter 1 I attempted to establish a conceptual framework for leadership development in the context of this relatively new research design. The application of the elements of art and principles of design to understanding the nature of leadership seems both a logical and natural progression. But the relationship has not been fully or completely articulated. Accordingly, I do not think it adequately understood. I do not presume to fill in all the blanks with this work, but I am confident that it might extend the conversation of how supervision might indeed be art.

It is Blumberg (1989) who sets the stage for much of my view of supervision as an art form, in his work *School Administration as a Craft*. Blumberg acknowledged that he wanted "to understand and explain (the craft of administration) in the context of the real-life world of the school administrator" and in so doing help the reader develop "the practice of craft" (p. 12) as a sort of habit of mind. Blumberg imagined that looking at the craft of supervision was only part of developing an enlarged view of life as a craft. This new view of teaching, leading, and learning was for him a significant psychological, emotional, and paradigmatic shift.

Drawing on Blumberg, Pajak, and Barone, I am offering a definition of the somewhat elusive challenge of seeing supervision as art form. Barone's (1998) research in some ways casts the longest shadow on my work, for it was Barone who framed Eisner's (1982; 1983) opinion that if we see teaching as art we can begin to see supervision of teaching as art as well. Barone frames the notion of supervision as an aesthetic dimension but notes that there is little consensus that teaching is an artlike activity. Given this reality, questions also remain about the advantages and disadvantages of seeing the supervision of teaching as aesthetic. My standpoint, conversely, is that viewing supervision as aesthetic enlarges our view of what effective teaching might become. Additionally, I suggest that the supervision-as-art metaphor allows us to see differently not only teaching but also the supervision of teaching.

I am quick to note that some writers find the notion of supervision as aesthetic or as art impractical and unrealistic (Oliva & Pawlas, 2004). Oliva & Pawlas state: "Practically, such artistic supervision would require a virtuoso performance that may be beyond the range of many persons who hold supervisory positions. The preparation of specialists who can tune into the varied nuances of teaching also poses a problem" (p. 380). My rejoinder to the wise and grounded comments of my detractors is this: If we fail to prepare supervisors of instruction with the tools, mechanisms, perspectives, and intellect for an enlarged understanding of teaching, we risk losing our very best teachers who yearn for a vocation that embraces their courage to do things differently. And when we continue to do supervision solely as inspection, data collection, and checklist, we risk deflating the soul of those teachers who see instruction as art and their curriculum as the canvas upon which students wholly engage in the full aesthetic of learning and of life.

CONCLUSIONS ON THE CONCEPTUAL BASIS FOR SUPERVISION AS ART

In my observation of art classrooms in elementary schools, I tend to find that most students see themselves as capable artists. When I work with student teachers in high school, I find that few of their students see themselves as skilled in much of anything. Somewhere along the journey from kindergarten to high school, the capacity for students to see life as an aesthetic experience is lost. I fear that part of the students' numbness that comes with years is the product of assessment-driven teaching. It is not the teachers' fault, for they are not often expected to do more than show results on tests, and this is important in part. But the fault lies with us all—policy makers, boards of education, school leadership, professors of supervision, teachers, and parents—because we acquiesce to the notion that good test results are the only goal. If we can begin recognizing that good teaching is indeed art and our supervision acknowledges this truth, we can begin helping our students to learn less about what is on the tests and more about life's aesthetic qualities that help us understand ourselves, others, our world. In my way of thinking, supervision as art recognizes, as Steinbeck (1955) noted, that "a great teacher is a great artist and that there are as few as there are any other great artists." I believe we are compelled to become great supervisors who recognize great teachers and the art that is their craft. Ideally, the process of seeing supervision through the elements of art and the principles of design will help us see and embrace teaching that is art.

QUESTIONS FOR DISCUSSION

1. Based on your experiences, how would you define supervision at your school?
2. Think about the times people observed your teaching. List three to five things about that observation that made you nervous.
3. Drawing from your answers in question 2 above, discuss in particular what it was that made you nervous. What feelings did you have? Where did those feelings come from?
4. What kinds of observations do you find most beneficial? Why?
5. List three to five things you dislike most about observations. What might you do to change these things so that they might be less bothersome or more helpful?
6. What kinds of feedback did you receive from your observations?
7. When you think about doing observations, what do you hope that teachers will say about your style, your visits, and your feedback?
8. What is your philosophy of supervision?

7

Elements of Art as Supervision

As described in chapter 3, the elements of art provide observers a fundamental language for describing art. The elements tend to be a specific, and often concrete, vocabulary for describing art. The elements are line, shape, value, form, space, color, and texture.

In leadership the elements let us create a view, a perception, and a vision of what schooling might be; frequently, within each school all seven elements are present. In matters of supervision the elements bring to both the observer and the teacher a mechanism for portraying the specific and aesthetic qualities of instruction. When traditional supervisory methodologies help establish what is observable and measurable, the elements of art for supervision help us begin to reflect on the nuances, the subtleties of successful classrooms. In a very specific way, these same elements give the instructor and instructional supervisor common language with which to discuss the lesson. For example, in one setting the element of form might have a larger role, relative to the perceptivity of the other elements in the classroom, in the teacher's construction of meaning and knowledge. The supervisor and teacher agree in the preconference that they will be paying particular attention to form, as they define it, in the observation. In the postobservation, then, the discussion focuses on that element. They both know what the focus is, they tend to it, and then they reflect on it. In that way, the supervisory function helps teacher and instructional leader to delve deeply in the nature of learning and teaching, not just on the outcomes of the lesson.

Realistically, however, there are certain facets of the supervisory process that are not aesthetic in nature. A very important part of the development of the elements of art for supervision, for example, is to recognize that before any discussion about the aesthetics of a lesson can occur, two conditions must be in place. First, in every lesson observed a primary focus must be on

the answer to the following question: Did the students achieve the learning outcomes? No matter the form or structure of the lesson, it is folly to discuss the art
of anything if no student learning has occurred. Second, in every lesson observed both teacher and observer must answer this question: Did the classroom
management support or impede the attainment of the learning outcomes?
Again, it would make little sense to observe a lesson and then begin discussing
the art of a teaching lesson when students were off task, sleeping, talking, or
something else was happening that interfered with the lesson.

After the first two questions are answered in the affirmative, and only then,
the instructional supervisor can begin to describe the observation by means
of the language of the elements of art for supervision. It might be on the order of discussing with someone the elements of his/her artwork before that
person has any opportunity to arrange for the painting or before that person
has even decided on a subject. In figure 7.1, I offer one example of a guide,
or checklist, I use when observing a lesson using the elements of art for su-

Figure 7.1.   Preconference: Elements of Supervision Checklist

Leader's Name: _____

Cycle: 1 2 3 _____

Teacher's Name: _____

Date of Conference: _____

Structure Needed (circle):   high   mixture   low

Directions: As you prepare for developing elements of art for supervision or principles of
design for supervision, consider the necessary conditions for supporting growth. Specifically, remember to acknowledge your current Conceptual Levels, Degrees of Disequilibrium, and Stages of Concern.

Step 1: Purpose
_____ Aesthetic focus:

○ review progress
○ select a new element
○ select a new principle

Notes: _____

_____

_____

_____

Step 2: Feelings about growth
_____ Conceptual level
_____ Disequilibrium
_____ Stage of concern

Notes: _____

_____

_____

_____

Figure 7.1. (*Continued*)

Step 3: Learning outcomes for observed teacher
_____ Learning outcomes stated
_____ Rationale for selection
_____ Evidence of listening
_____ Lesson plan or outline reviewed

Notes: _____

_____

_____

_____

Step 4: Classroom management for observed teacher
_____ Strategies/concerns shared
_____ Rationale for selection
_____ Evidence of listening

Notes: _____

_____

_____

_____

Step 5: Element of art for supervision
_____ Element selection and definition
_____ Rationale for selection
_____ Evidence of performance

Notes: _____

_____

_____

_____

Step 6: Principle of design for supervision
_____ Principle selection and definition
_____ Rationale for selection
_____ Evidence of performance

Notes: _____

_____

_____

_____

Step 7: Follow-up
_____ Feedback time
_____ Self-analysis/reflection sheet
_____ Closing comments

pervision and the principles of design for supervision. You will note that steps 3 (learning outcomes) and 4 (classroom management) come before the discussion of the element. In fact, if either 3 or 4 are not successful, we do not even discuss the element.

With all these pieces in place, we can begin to work with the supervisory function from an artistic perspective while simultaneously imagining how we might help our teachers develop more fully in their classrooms. But we cannot develop supervision in the absence of the teaching process. In other words, as we provide instructional leadership and help the teacher, we also engage in self-evaluation of our own ability to use the elements to think in new and exciting ways about the nature of supervision. Also, as we discuss with our teacher the lesson or the event, we are practicing the aesthetic that Dewey (1934) imagined (see chapter 1), in which we assign values and make judgments about our experiences. Both the teacher and the instructional supervisor have the bidirectional benefit of the aesthetic experience—and that aesthetic is much of what art is.

I will organize this chapter as I did chapter 3, defining the element, offering an artist's view, and using the scenario. These three pieces are the same as found in the leadership section of the text. I hope that by comparing the leadership perspectives in chapter 3 to the supervisory perspectives below, we may be able to discover distinctions as well as similarities.

AUTUMN WILLOW #1, 2000

Acryllic, charcoal, India ink on paper, 50 × 40 in.
Collection of Reynolds-Dewalt Printing Inc., New Bedford, MA

Element No. 1

Line: A long narrow mark or stroke made on or in a surface.

The Artist's View

Artists recognize the important contribution line brings to a holistic understanding of a given work. Lines can be vertical, horizontal, diagonal, curvilinear, or zigzagged. When artists vary the line's length, width, texture, direction, or degree of curve, they can multiply the visual impact of a work of art. For example, vertical lines convey height and inactivity. Vertical lines also express stability, dignity, poise, stiffness, and formality. Imagine how vertical lines on the side of a building will make the building look taller, more stable. By contrast, horizontal lines are static. They express peace, rest,

quiet, and stability. Horizontal lines can help make one feel content, relaxed, and calm. Diagonal and zigzag lines suggest activity. They communicate action, movement, and tension. Diagonal lines also seem to work against gravity and create a pull and tension that can be uncomfortable. Curved lines also express activity. Spiral curves around a central point are hypnotic and tend to draw the eye to the center. Zigzag lines in an artwork help to create a feeling of confusion. Clearly, an element as simple as line can have a powerful effect on the message of an artwork.

Line as a Case Study

The principal at Sharing Elementary School wants to implement shared decision making with her staff. She has come to believe that by doing so she can support the site-based planning that the central office values as a part of the accreditation process. More specifically, the principal recognizes that shared decision making would be an important part of the school improvement plan. The question arises, however, as to where to begin with this process.

The principal decides first to implement an interview committee for selecting new teachers. She asks teacher leaders from each grade level to select two representatives for participation in the committee. One member is the primary participant, while the other is the alternate. The teachers are keenly excited about this opportunity to be involved in an important part of the school business. The interview team meets with the personnel director for legal guidelines and to develop an appropriate list of interview questions. The personnel office forwards applications for the committee's review. The committee selects five teachers for a formal interview.

The interviews go as scheduled. The teachers have open conversations about the merits of this candidate in light of another candidate. Finally, the team makes the tough decision to hire a certain teacher. The committee forwards the selection to the principal. Several days later, at an open board meeting, the superintendent recommends to the board a different teacher to receive a contract. Word gets back to the interview committee. The teachers demand to see the principal.

Upon meeting the principal, the team discovers that the principal had meant the group to help with interviews but felt no obligation to follow its recommendation. In fact, the principal thought the team's choice was a poor one and so had recommended someone else. The teachers leave the meeting frustrated and demoralized. What had once seemed to be an open opportunity for shared decision making became another moment when the distance between the principal's office and the teachers' rooms exceeded the physical space.

In this scenario, the fault is not that the principal made the decision. Nor is it unrealistic for the teachers to be angered. What was missing in the process was as an honest discussion about the role of the interview team in the selection process. If the principal did not feel obligated to accept the team's recommendatio, that was certainly reasonable. The team did not understand the negotiable lines, the boundaries and limits of its mission and resulting decisions. If the teachers had known that their recommendation was only that, a recommendation, the nature of the relationship would have been clear. The team would have known what was expected. Its members could have appreciated the invitation to be a part of the decision making but would have realized that ultimately the principal would have to make the decision regarding employment matters.

A Supervision Perspective

Line as an element of the art of supervision helps us consider boundaries, responsibilities, and limits. Indeed, a successful instructional leader communicates the nature of the relationship with which he/she is involved. As I have said previously, so much of what we do in schooling is relational in nature—student to teacher, teacher to principal, student and teacher to curriculum, school to community—and this reality is even more true when it involves instructional supervision.

Successful instructional supervisors, at the outset, define the relationship with the other person. The supervisor addresses questions like, "What can we expect of each other?" or "How will we communicate expectations, concerns, questions?" or "How will we plan our meeting dates and times?" My experience tells me that supervision fails most often when the lines are not clear.

The lines may create space between, connect, or surround people. If the element of line is a focus for supervision, we can know that the emphasis for successful supervision in this case is clarity about roles and responsibilities, for the instructional leaders as well as the people with whom they work. When we are clear about our roles relative to supervision, we reduce the hurtful and frustrating moments that come with misinformation and mistakes. And even more importantly, the use of line helps build an atmosphere of trust and openness that comes with authentic and genuine communication.

TARGET PRACTICE NO. 5, 1994

From the series "Target Practice Take This Take That"
Charcoal on paper, 50 × 40 in.
Collection of Kimberly Kelly, Bedford Hills, NY

Element No. 2

Value: The lightness or darkness of a color or object.

The Artist's View

Value is the art element that describes the relative darkness or lightness of an object in a drawing or painting. How much value a surface has depends on how much light is reflected. If there is an absence of light, the surface will be dark; if there is much light, the surface becomes lighter. There are many ways that artists create value. For example, when one looks at a dollar bill, one may see an entire artwork composed of tiny lines. The artist or the engraver uses lines to create value. The closer and more plentiful the lines appear in a space, the darker the value. In turn, the less line in a given space, the less value, and the lighter the space appears. In fact, value is related to all the elements and is often understood best in association with other elements.

Value as a Case Study

At Florence High School, the principal, Mike Angelo, proclaims that the arts are a central focus for creating productive citizens. He made a PowerPoint

presentation at the last PTO meeting about arts in the school. Just this morning, however, Mr. Angelo received a memo from the district finance director
that he was to cut next year's school budget by 5 percent. Also, based on recent directives from the state department, all principals were to place special
emphasis on the basics. The superintendent stated, "Student test scores simply must improve or we will be placed on probation and we do not need that
publicity!"

Mr. Angelo calls in Mr. Drum, Ms. Shakespeare, and Ms. Pallette and informs them that since they all have less than three years' experience in the
district, he will have to let them go at the end of the year. When Ms. Pallette,
the art teacher, asks why Mr. Gridiron, who has been with the system only
two years, is not being released, the principal states, "The community is not

going to tolerate losing the football coach who just returned from an exciting college experience at Football A&M. Anyway, he is one of Florence High's most famous graduates."

When we say that we value academics and the arts but our actions communicate something very different, the message is lost. In essence, our articulated values are inconsistent with our daily practices. This type of disconnect can destroy teacher morale, communicate dangerous messages to students, and confuse our purpose for schooling. The light of our message becomes lost behind the shadows of our actions. Although the example is ridiculous at one level, many of us know of examples that echo this story.

A Supervision Perspective

Given that value represents the "light" that emerges from our daily activities and that light directs our attention to what matters most, school leaders can confuse what is pressing with what is really important. In other words, what is currently clearest or brightest might not be nearly as important as something that lies in the shadows. In terms of supervision, then, we use value to help us remember that what a teacher does in the classroom emerges from the "shadows," or background, of that teacher's cultural influences. From experiences as distant as childhood to others as recent as this morning at home, our experiences affect our ability to see the relative values in our daily lives. The same holds true for the supervisor's capacity to see what is obvious and what is subtle.

Probably most important for supervision is helping our teachers to avoid being blinded by the most pressing burdens of the day and thus losing sight of the less obvious but more important demands that come with teaching. For example, when a new teacher becomes overwhelmed with all the new demands placed on him/her, the greatest value in supervision is in taking time to listen to the concerns, trying to identify emotions, and then assisting in developing specific actions plans for addressing the needs. Our perspective as an observer might be useful in helping the teacher discern the competing values of the moment. Critically, however, supervision as art does not try to "fix" the teacher's problem. Rather, the supervisor who understands the element of value helps a teacher to place the competing events' emotions into categories of most important and pressing (light) and less important and "can wait" (dark).

Let us consider the experienced teacher who is new to the district and is losing control of his emotions when dealing with children. When I sat with him to discuss the particulars of his classroom management, it became clear to me through active listening that the problem was not so much with the children or his classroom management. This teacher had so much emotion wrapped up inside that he was reacting to colleagues and students in disproportionate ways. A student had asked him a question about a math problem, and the teacher had responded, "You dummy. I told you that answer twice already." Later, when a teacher asked him about the incident, the teacher had snapped, "These kids are just plain sorry and the principal does not give a flip about what teachers need." In this exchange, it became clear to me that there was much more going on than just what was most recent and brightest (i.e., light value). During a later conversation I learned the teacher had moved to the district for only one reason, and that was to look after his ailing parents. He was angry, saddened, confused, and exhausted. Through listening actively I came to understand the background (dark values) events that were playing a destructive role in his life. These very important personal matters, although less obvious upon first examination, were affecting his professional performance.

If, then, we recognize that value represents the gradations of light to dark in viewing the "picture" of a person, supervision can assist teachers to reflect on their own lives to tease out the most obvious and demanding parts of life that are competing with the less noticeable but equally demanding elements.

NOCTURNE FOR HEATHER, 1991

From the series "Life with Heaher"
Ink wash on paper, 24⁷⁄₁₆ × 19¹¹⁄₁₆ in.
Collection of Smith Glassen, Providence, RI

Element No. 3

Shape: Two-dimensional area.

The Artist's View

A shape is a two-dimensional area that is defined in some certain way. By drawing an outline of a circle on a piece of paper, one has created a shape. By painting a solid red square, one has also created a shape. Shapes may be either free-form or geometric. Free-form shapes are uneven and irregular, and they usually promote a pleasant and soothing feeling. Geometric shapes, on the other hand, are stiff and uniform, generally suggesting organization and management with little or no emotion. Shape tends to appeal more to viewers' minds than to their emotions.

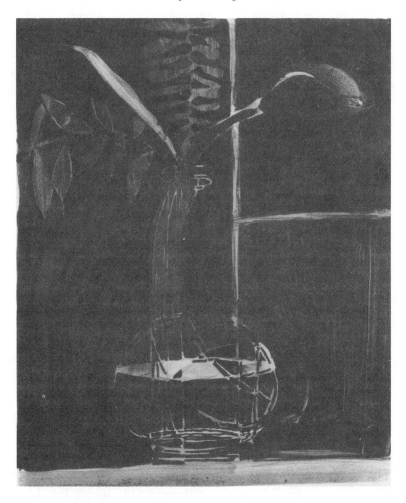

Shape as a Case Study

It is a typical first week of school for the principal at Round About Elementary. The principal has no idea how typical it is, because it is her first year in the position. On Monday, the school buses were late; one bus arrived 45 minutes after the start of school. On Tuesday, the cafeteria workers informed her that the ovens were not working and that there would be no lunch that day. On Wednesday, she was met at the door by Ms. Rookie, the new teacher, who had lost her keys to the classroom and proceeded to inform the principal, "I simply can not work with Ms. Parapro. She is no help at all. I need you to find me someone else." Also, the principal hears from the central office that the students will be eating sack lunches all week as the repair in the kitchen is going to take some time. Wednesday afternoon she is about to leave for the day when a student shows up at her door. She had ridden the bus home, found no one there, and walked back to school to find help. Thursday the finance director arrives to go over the revised budget and reminds the principal that there is no money for staff development this year. Friday morning there is an IEP meeting, and the Director of Special Education is at a conference. The superintendent wants to go over her expectations for the coming year today. Also, the reading material has yet to arrive from the publisher; the third-grade teachers want to know what to do for next week's instruction. Shortly after lunch, the principal receives a message from a local Evangelical Congregation of the United States and they need to use the facility over the weekend for church services.

Welcome to the world of management of school programs. A leader's ability to come to terms with the competing demands of school necessarily and directly affects the school's ability to offer a safe, orderly learning environment.

A Supervision Perspective

Instructional supervision seeks to develop a teacher's capacity to help students learn. But also at work in supervision are other factors in the classroom that affect student learning. Instruction is central and key to all learning. Planning, managing, budgeting, conferencing, testing, and scheduling are examples of what supervision as art also addresses in helping teachers be successful. These are examples of shape. I like to think of shape in supervision as everything that goes into teaching well, except instruction. But what might that list include?

In order for teachers to begin asking questions about student learning, they must address concerns that are personal. In other words, before I can ask how my students are doing, I have to be clear about how I am doing myself. It is not usual for teachers to put themselves first. It is just not in the composition of good teachers. They are accustomed to putting themselves, their needs, their health, and even their own families behind the needs of their students. But I suggest that such a priority, although sustainable for a short while, will ultimately result in ineffective instruction and teacher burnout.

This type of prioritizing is where shape as an element of artistic supervision emerges. Supervisors who recognize the role of shape in successful teaching pay particular attention, especially early in the school year, to making teachers comfortable with their surroundings. This comfort might come from answers to questions like: "What time do I have to be at school, and when should I leave?" or "Where do I park, and where is the bathroom?" or "How do I make copies, and how many copies can I make?" My mother, a professional educator for 30+ years, reminded me that if I did nothing else I should introduce my new teachers to three people: the custodian, the front office secretary, and the media specialist. Is this instruction? No, of course not. But we can be certain that if teachers are not comfortable with the basic management challenges of schooling, they are not likely to be comfortable knowing what students need.

Before the children arrive at the beginning of the school year, supervisors would do well to offer their teachers a basic orientation to the departments, the schools, the districts, and the community. I remember offering our new teachers a school-bus ride through the community from where their children came—what a powerful awakening when teachers understood more fully their children's neighborhoods. A different level of orientation to help teachers in the management of schooling involved getting them out of systemwide orientations and into their classrooms. There is a certain amount of paperwork that all new employees should complete before the children arrive. But what we found particularly useful was to have mentor teachers meet their new teachers at lunch on the second day of orientation. After lunch, the mentors would take the new teachers to their respective schools and provide an orientation to the physical plant and then deliver them to their classrooms. More than almost anything else, teachers want to get to their classrooms so they can set up for the children. Essentially, helping them get to the classrooms so that they can begin managing their new worlds is the whole point behind shape as a function of artistic supervision.

NIGHT GAMES, 2001

From the portfolio "Out at Home: Negro Baseball League, Volume II"
Suite of 12 prints, including 3 pages of text, 9 images
Lithograph, 20 × 15 in.
Courtesy, Ellen Sragow Gallery, New York

Element No. 4

Form: Three-dimensional structure or shape; geometric or free-form.

The Artist's View

Forms are shapes that are three-dimensional and are either geometric or free-form. In two-dimensional works of art—that is, artwork that hangs on a wall—artists use value on a shape to create a form. In other words, when artists add value to the shape of a circle, the shape becomes a sphere and takes on the illusion of a something that is three-dimensional, a form. Today artists refer to the lights and darks of a work of art as modeling or shading. Very dark areas of forms tend to recede into the artwork, where very light areas appear closest to the viewer. In three-dimensional art such as sculpture, all shapes are forms, because they take up space in three dimensions. True forms occupy height, width, and depth in space.

Form as a Case Study

The parents of Marjorie Settle come to you, the middle school principal, to complain because Marjorie has received a "zero" for a report in her social studies class. Her sixth-grade teacher had given the following directions regarding the assignment: "Your topic must be decent, researchable, and approved by me. You must have at least four bibliographic references in your report. Obtain my approval for your topic before proceeding." Six weeks after receiving this assignment, Marjorie was given a big fat goose-egg for her report on Jesus Christ. Marjorie had on at least five occasions attempted to obtain approval for her report from the teacher, but had been denied each time. The teacher had denied Marjorie's topic for two reasons: concern that the topic would foster an Establishment Clause violation and Marjorie's insistence that a single bibliographic reference, the Bible, was adequate for her research.

When we recognize the important role that perspective has for understanding a given situation, we also see the real importance that empathy has for successful leadership. Empathy is the capacity to understand and identify another person's feelings or difficulties. In the case study above, the principal clearly needs to support the teacher but also recognize the motivation and perspective of the student. As the principal communicates to the teacher the different levels of issues included in this potentially emotional decision, he can simultaneously communicate trust and commitment through the effective use of communication. In so doing, emotions can be addressed so that reason might prevail.

A Supervision Perspective

As I mentioned in chapter 3, the difference in management and leadership is the movement from shape to form, from two-dimensional perspective to a three-dimensional one. If supervision is to be art, maybe the most important element is this notion of form. Form as an element of supervision as art involves empathy. And by empathy I want to emphasize that I am speaking of both the supervisor's and the teacher's capacity to understand or feel another person's perspective.

There are a number of ways in which we can develop empathy as a skill for supervision. Probably the most effective and most revealing way to analyze our listening skills is to tape conversations we have family, with children, with colleagues, or with anyone else who will participate. When we listen to our tapes, we can begin to recognize ways we interrupt conversation. Or we may find that we encourage discussion. Or we might discover methods of active listening that communicate to the speaker that we are hearing what he/she is saying. Whatever we might find out about our listening skills, I have come to realize that virtually no one, when I pose the question about their listening skills, admits to being a poor listener. Disturbingly, in fact, I find that the people who profess to be the best listeners are often the poorest practitioners. So, the first step toward embracing the element of form in the context of the art of supervision is to take time to listen to ourselves, to reflect on our own practice.

One instrument that might help with this self-assessment is figure 7.2, a type of score sheet I have used in mentoring courses. Basically, the score sheet breaks conversation down into two categories. Above the line are examples of behavior that support conversation. Below the line are examples of ways we can interrupt or disrupt conversation. (See also appendix E.)

As we listen to our tapes, each time we find examples of the categories above, we make note of that moment and try to quote the example. At the

Figure 7.2. Active Listening Score Sheet

Paraphrase feelings accurately (+50)—The listener makes a statement labeling the feeling he/she heard in the statement. This is the highest form of listening.

Paraphrase content accurately (+20)—The listener repeats the content of what he/she has just heard in his/her own words.

Door openers (+10)—"Tell me more . . ."; "Sounds interesting . . ."

Acknowledgement responses (+10)—"uh huh"; "yes"; "right"; "certainly."

Nonverbal encouragement (+10)—The listener looks at the person; nods head, leans forward.

Roadblocks (−5)—Directing, threatening, preaching, lecturing, providing answers, disapproving, sympathizing.

Hooking Statements (−10)—Each person in the conversation uses one thought from what the other person has just said and then hooks in his/her own thoughts.

Ships passing in the night (−20)—Each person talks about his/her own thoughts without giving any indication he/she has heard what the other person has said.

Nonverbal discouragement (−30)—The listener frowns, turns back, yawns.

Total +'s _____ − Total −'s _____ = Score _____
© Zach Kelehear, 2004

end of the tape, we go back to tally our examples. The first step in growing is in understanding where we need to develop. This active listening process allows for such assessment.

As I remind my classes, it is not always practical or advisable to encourage conversation. Sometimes we simply do best by discouraging conversation. I am reminded of the time a group of my student teachers were lamenting the woes of working in the middle school in rural South Carolina. It was clear that no positive benefit could come from such bickering and fussing at the school site. But when these same students arrived at the weekly seminar, I was prepared to encourage more conversation about conditions at the school that had clearly begun to affect these students. At the school, continued conversation was not appropriate, but at the seminar, continued conversation was entirely appropriate; there we were able to develop a deeper understanding of what was going on at the school that so profoundly frustrated these students.

Form as a part of the art of supervision has as its most powerful tool the use of empathy. Empathy, when done well, allows us to hear both the content and the feelings in a message. When I am able to hear what your surface message is as well as any embedded messages, I am becoming an artist of form for effective supervision.

NIGHT FISH, 1993

From the series "Strange Fruit"
Lithograph, 22 × 12 in.
Collection of the artist

Element No. 5

Space: Area around, between, above, below, or within an object.

The Artist's View

All the area that exists around, between, above, below, and within an object is considered to be space. Forms and shapes are considered to be "positive" space; space that occupies the area in and around the form and shape is called "negative" space. Artists who utilize large negative spaces may express loneliness or freedom. Crowding together positive space reflects tension or togetherness. Depending on each other, positive and negative spaces interact with one another to create meaning. Space in three dimensions is the area that is over, under, around, behind, and through. Sculpture, jewelry, ar-

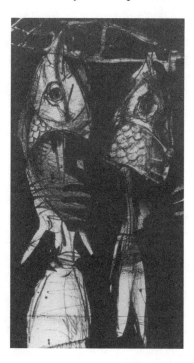

chitecture, weaving, and ceramics are three-dimensional art forms. They produce art that takes up real space.

Space as a Case Study

As a new teacher, Mr. Protégé has the benefit of working with Ms. Mentor. Mr. Protégé came highly recommended on the basis of his academic achievement. He is described as earnest, hardworking, and extremely conscientious. He dresses very neatly and is polite almost to a fault. He teaches a question-and-answer method almost exclusively. Mr. Protégé says that the children (sixth-graders) have to learn the facts before they can interpret and that he hopes that everyone will master the material in the lesson plan. He follows his lesson plan literally.

In a meeting with Ms. Mentor, Mr. Protégé appears with a notebook and asks at least 25 questions about methods. He carefully writes down the answers. In between his questions about methods, he asks about certification, and he appears confused about what he is expected to do as a first-year teacher. He is very serious and rarely shows humor. He exhibits little awareness of feelings.

Mr. Protégé is like many first-year teachers who feel overwhelmed by the seemingly unending demands that come their way. Allowing him space to grow but not allowing him to be alone is a difficult balance for school leadership. In order for young teachers to grow to higher levels of effectiveness, however, effective supervision needs to understand the role of support and challenge in creating space for professional development.

A Supervision Perspective

The use of positive and negative space creates support and balance in a classroom. When we work in instructional supervision, I imagine that the positive space—or most obvious points of observation—we see includes learning outcomes and classroom management. These two pieces of a successful classroom are what we must see first when observing the art of the instruction. They ought to be primary. It is not that other characteristics are unimportant. In fact, matters such as providing positive reinforcement, encouraging high-order questions, or delivering cues and feedback can be essential parts of a successful lesson. But our ability, or our necessity, to distinguish positive and negative space in a lesson rests in a teacher's ability to handle the information.

For example, a first-year teacher who is new to a community carries an enormous amount of what the psychologist Jean Piaget calls disequilibrium (what I call stress). Because of the competing and overwhelming demands that come with being new to a position and to a community, this teacher will likely have difficulty in assuming many responsibilities. More specifically, when an instructional leader observes the lesson, he/she would do well to limit the points of observation to learning outcomes and classroom management. These two areas are most important, and we communicate this emphasis on positive space to the new teacher. Importantly, we are limiting the observation points in the positive space to be observed. There are still negative-space points (ones in the background, or not the focus) that are happening, but to ask the new teacher to consider them all would be unrealistic and unfair.

From a broader perspective, in the case study above we find that the mentor would do well to not confuse positive space for negative space. Put differently, the mentor will respond to the protégé in a way that acknowledges what she can handle or manage. In this case, limiting the focus to the positive space will be helpful, for the protégé will be able to address a limited number of items. In much the same way, instructional supervision is a process of telling our teachers what we consider positive space, what we want to see first, and then being certain that our observation echoes that commitment. If, as we agreed, we enter the room to observe learning outcomes and classroom management (positive space) but then focus on the excellent decorations in the room or the teacher's messy desk or the arrangement of desks (negative space), we risk confusing what we say we believe and what our actions "say" we believe. Both positive and negative spaces play important roles in creating a valuable learning experience for teacher, for students, and for instructional leaders. But the key for supervision is to match the positive and negative space to the needs and skills of the teacher—not too much, not too little, but just enough to stretch the teacher to grow without overwhelming him.

SPANISH GARDEN NO. VI, 1994-1995

From the series "Spanish Gardens"
Acrylic on paper, 30 × 22 in.
Collection of Dr. and Mrs. William Tsiaras, Barrington, RI

Element No. 6

Color: Property of objects coming from reflected light.

The Artist's View

Color is the most dynamic and exciting element of art. It is also the hardest element to describe. Color comes from reflected light. When light reflects off of an object such as a red ball, the red ball absorbs all light waves except the red light waves. The red light waves reflect into our eyes and are interpreted by our brain as the color red. Often, we represent colors along a spectrum—primary (red, yellow, and blue), secondary (violet, green, and orange), and tertiary or intermediate (red orange, red violet, blue violet, blue green, yellow green, yellow orange). When these spectral colors are bent into a circle, we form a color wheel. White and black are not considered colors at all. Black is the absence of color, and white is considered to be a combination of all colors.

Color as a Case Study

Mr. Collaboration, superintendent of the local school district, enjoys having teachers work together on systemwide projects. He believes that the more he involves people in decision making, the more likely they are to get along and help create a positive learning environment for students. In attempting to select various people for participation in the projects, Mr.

Collaboration wonders if it might be best to put together people with similar personality types or if it might be best to mix styles within groups.

The curriculum committee, however, concerns Mr. Collaboration. The Assistant Superintendent for Instruction, who has been in the district for 31 years, leads this committee and clearly has a special reading program she wants the school board to adopt. Her leadership style tends to intimidate members of her committee. Additionally, she is not likely to embrace differing perspectives, and there is gossip that she can make life tough on teachers who disagree with her.

Mr. Collaboration has a special challenge before him: How can he encourage the assistant superintendent to be more open to others' ideas? How might he pressure her to change her leadership style without being guilty of what he is accusing her of doing to other teachers? In a broader sense, then,

Mr. Collaboration wants a culture of openness and collaboration, but some of his important leaders do not agree with his perspective.

A Supervision Perspective

As different colors might contribute to the beauty of a painting, different teaching styles can add color and vibrancy to a school. Using color in the art of supervision is about celebrating the diversity of teaching styles. Encouraging different teaching styles can help teachers respond to different kinds and needs of students. But providing for diversity of teaching styles just for the sake of allowing diversity, without meeting the needs of students, does not make much sense.

Effective supervision helps teachers know their students well. Teachers should know something about their student's families and neighborhoods. They should know something about their interests. And they should know something about how they learn best. Given this knowledge, the effective teacher works to craft lessons that speak to the interests and predispositions of the students. This is not to say, however, that the curriculum and teacher are to become simply whatever the student needs. Rather, it is to say that teachers can vary their pedagogies in such a way as to create a bridge by which students can connect to a curriculum and vice versa. This is where the art of supervision uses the element of color to help match and blend the student, the teacher, and the curriculum. Just as one might mix colors to yield a different shade or tint, instructional supervisors can help teachers mix and match pedagogy to students in order that teachers might present a curriculum that is meaningful, relevant, and powerful.

TURQUOISE AUTUMN, 1998–1999

Acrylic on canvas, 59 × 39 in.
Collection of Kirk and Karen Sykes, Boston, MA

Element No. 7

Texture: Feel or appearance of an object or surface.

The Artist's View

Texture is the art element that refers to how things feel or look as if they might feel. We perceive texture through touch and vision. One can use tactile sensitivity by using skin receptors to feel texture, but one can also experience visual texture by looking at the illusion of a three-dimensional

surface. Once again, the element of value comes to the forefront. Without the relative lightness and darkness of the surface arrangement, the illusion of a surface texture could not be seen. Texture is important to every art medium.

Texture as a Case Study

Over the last ten years, the ethnicity of Homogeneous School District has changed radically. Because of a booming labor market in the area, there has been an expansion of migrant and immigrant labor in the community. As a result, the school population of the district has changed from predominantly white to predominantly minority. The white parents are expressing a growing concern over the educational quality of their children amid the district's attempt to address the special needs of students with limited English skills. As superintendent of the district you see clearly that this is not the case. You imagine that what is probably happening is that the white community is using academic quality as a "code" phrase for their discomfort with different students. They want their children to remain in classes with other white students, segregated from the growing presence of the minority group.

Your challenge is to embrace the "newcomers" without alienating the "old guard." In what ways might the district bring the two groups together in a celebration of diversity and academic excellence?

A Supervision Perspective

When students from different cultures, different genders, or different backgrounds move into groups or "cliques," the fabric of the school culture can begin to unravel. Certainly instructional supervisors has a special responsibility to prevent such divisions. In a similar and disturbing way, teachers too can begin to form cliques. Balkanization of the teaching staff can create all types of destructive forces. Although my first thoughts in terms of examples move toward high schools, I fear that no school levels are free from such a danger. I can remember several schools where divisions between staffs were a real problem. The English departments and history departments rarely spoke. The coaches of athletics stayed near the gym. The fine arts department stayed in its wing of the building. The administrative staff seemed rarely to leave the front office. At an elementary school, the kindergarten teachers and second-grade teachers hardly knew each other. The elementary school principal first began to recognize this division when she brought the grade-level chairs together to discuss vertical planning and had to introduce them to each other!

One of the real challenges for instructional supervision to find a way to bring varying teaching staffs together. Obviously, the real beneficiaries of such cohesion will be the students, for they will begin to see learning more holistically and in a less compartmentalized way. In order to create a shared vision of instruction, the instructional leader would do well to build bridges between departments. For example, the instructional leader begins to coordinate opportunities for teachers to observe within their departments. Teachers begin to see the exciting, and sometimes not exciting, things going on in their departments. Just being aware of each other's subjects and pedagogies helps create common places for shared interest and conversation.

After finding ways to observe within the departments or grade levels, the instructional supervisor can begin structuring interdepartmental visits and observations. I emphasize that the leadership structures the visits, because it can be very difficult for teachers to schedule common times or find substitutes. When initiatives are inconvenient, they often fail. The

instructional leader also may provide observation sheets that help in seeing the story in the classroom. Maybe all teachers can agree, with the guidance of the instructional leader, that an observation will focus on one
strategy or one management style and that at each faculty meeting teachers will be asked to describe something they saw in their observations
about which they were excited. What transpires is that teachers come to
know each other more fully; teachers get into the habit of finding good
things going on; and students get to see teachers as learning and developing. In the end, the fabric of our varied staffs begins to come together
into a texture of diverse teaching styles bound together by a shared commitment to teaching excellence.

CONCLUSION ON THE ELEMENTS OF INSTRUCTIONAL SUPERVISION

The elements of art for supervision provide us with some very specific
directions for supporting quality instruction. Line, value, shape, form,
space, color, and texture may all, individually or collectively, support
quality instruction. By using the models above as points of departure but
not being limited by them, we can begin to acknowledge that supervision
can be more than formula. It can be an art of knowing how to lead teachers along exciting paths for student learning. Teachers and instructional
leaders have a common language, and in that language the variability and
variety that comes with effective teaching is honored. And in our dance to
understand the complex and daunting challenge of helping students
learn, we can learn to let the elements of art lead us in our dance of supervision.

QUESTIONS FOR DISCUSSION

1. Given the seven elements of supervision listed in this chapter, which
   one(s) do you feel most comfortable with as an instructional leader?
   Why?
2. As an instructional leader, which element do you lack command of?
   What might be some specific strategies for developing that element?
3. Identify one element that you believe would be useful for an instructional leader and design a staff development program for your school
   where you could introduce and develop that element.
4. Reflect on current realities at your school setting and identify one problem as an area for growth. Develop an action plan that uses one or
   more of the elements to facilitate your school's effort to address that

problem. In your action plan, remember to identify a specific goal, some potential obstacles, a timetable, and an assessment of your level of success.

5. Select one of the case studies and apply the following "Art of Leadership Critique." Remember to describe what happened, analyze particular behaviors, find meaning, and evaluate the leadership.

Art of Leadership Critique
Topic/Issue at Hand:_____
Leader Name:_____
School/System Setting:_____
Date:_____

Step 1: Description
The goal is to describe objectively what you see; to delay judgment. List system, leader, date; describe setting and key players; identify central or core issue; identify elements of leadership that are present.
A description might include: _____

_____

_____

Step 2: Analysis
The goal is to describe behaviors of what you see. Describe how the elements listed in step 1 use the principles of leadership. Which principles provide organization for the elements? List your emotional reaction to these factors. How does the leadership strategy make you feel? How does it make others feel?
The analysis might include: _____

_____

_____

Step 3: Interpretation
The goal is to find meaning in what you see. Does it work? Why? What do you think the leader is trying to do? What is the goal? What are the symbolic goals that emerge? What do they mean?
One interpretation might be: _____

_____

_____

Step 4: Judgment
The goal is to evaluate what you see. How could the leader have been more successful? Who benefits from the decisions? Who does not?

What balance is there between what the leader says, what he does, and what he believes? What is the relationship between what the school values, believes, and does?

A possible judgment would include: _____

_____

_____

8

Principles of Design as Supervision

Principles of design are the rules that govern how artists organize the elements of art. In matters of supervision, the principles can generate school-wide and systemwide solutions rather than addressing specific or classroom issues. Another way of imagining it is that the principles offer the cohesive force that helps the elements build synergy rather than separate energies. Principles of design are the organizing forces that help extend meaning for combinations of elements or art. It is important to note that by allowing principles of design to guide all observations and teaching units, thus building unity across the school, individual teachers free themselves to call on various elements to meet the needs of their students and the curriculum, thus allowing for creativity and flexibility. The principles of design are emphasis, rhythm, movement, balance, proportion, variety, and harmony/unity.

For supervision, just as in the leadership discussion in chapter 4, the principles of design are the organizing and philosophical guides to making decisions daily, weekly, and yearly. They tend to be applicable across the school or district, not only in the classroom. They are not specific answers to specific questions, although they could be. Rather, they are themes or core values that we articulate. In so doing, we can make more direct and event-specific decisions, with one or more of the principles offering us a vision for where we want to go.

BOUQUET FOR NANCY, 1996

From the series "Urban Memoirs"
Suite of 7, 2nd state
Lithograph on paper, 36 × 26 in.
Collection of Nancy Phillips, Newport, RI

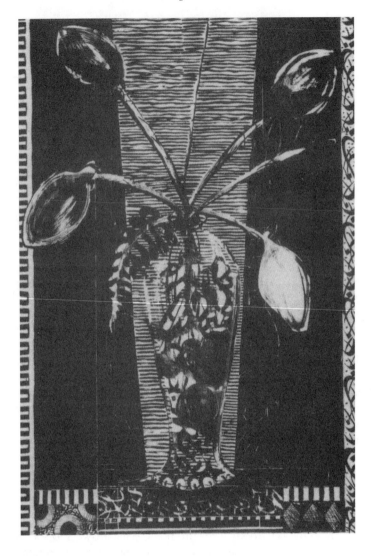

Principle No. 1

Emphasis: one part of a work is dominant over the other parts. The element noticed first is dominant; the elements noticed later are subordinate.

The Artist's View

When we talk about emphasis, we are recognizing a particular element that stands out in an artwork. For example, as we view an abstract painting our first reaction might be one of confusion. Upon closer examination, however, we begin notice certain colors or shapes that tend to dominate the painting. We also notice that other elements, such as line or shape, are present but not as obvious. In this way the observer begins to conceptualize and organize the painting's meaning through the use of emphasis.

Emphasis as a Case Study

At Brookhaven Elementary School, the principal is interested in communicating an inclusive philosophy in his rapidly changing school zone. Over the past five years, children from as many as nine different countries have joined his school. These newcomers add to an already fluid cultural setting where 12 distinct countries are already represented.

The principal has utilized all seven elements of effective leadership but decided to pay special attention to texture as a dominant theme in the school. Surrounding the American flag at the entrance of the school are flags for each country represented by his children. Every hall has a different art theme. Different classes are responsible for developing a concept, painting it, and displaying it in identified areas throughout the school. Outside the school, in the back at the playground, all walls are awash with painted histories of countries. He likes to think of this area as graffiti with a purpose! Each month a cultural Olympics is held, where sports and pastimes from various countries are studied, practiced, and played. The dining hall offers theme weeks where menus reveal cultural influences. Corresponding to the dining themes are dress code themes. Instead of falling into the struggle of enforcing a dress code, the principal imagines that the theme weeks might actually help create a positive and exciting environment in his school. And finally, during the summer with staff development funds, the principal calls in lead teachers from the various grades to organize the curriculum scope and sequence from kindergarten to grade five. The teachers develop themes around which reading, mathematics, science, social studies, art, music, and physical education can create units of study. For example, during Mexico week a visitor finds that students in all grades, in all subject areas, are studying their subjects with Mexico as the major theme. The basics are still the focus. Teachers and students still recognize that they need to do well on standardized tests. But amid the important work of schooling, the principal emphasizes the leadership element of texture as a way to celebrate the children that were his school.

A Supervision Perspective

Conducting supervision under the guidance of the principle of emphasis suggests a certain type of observation for all teachers throughout the school. Relying on the theme that emphasis might concentrate more heavily on one element or another, an instructional leader might have teachers at all grade levels and subject areas focus on the refinement of texture, color, shape, form, value, line, or space in each of their lessons. Assuming for a moment that the instructional leader is conducting observations with the elements in mind, he/she might encourage teachers throughout the school to focus on the development of the element of texture. In different settings or classrooms the use and understanding of texture will likely differ widely. Such variance would certainly be in keeping with the notion of teaching as art.

Let us reflect for a moment on the school in the above case study. The principle of design that provides guidance and direction is emphasis. In this case, texture is the element chosen to reflect the principle of emphasis, in part because it serves to embrace and celebrate the diversity of student backgrounds. The instructional leader shares with the teachers that, because emphasis is the principle for all decisions across the curriculum and because texture is the element to be focused on, all successful lessons should be built around finding ways to celebrate the diversity among the student body. The teachers conduct lessons utilizing one or more of the elements, but they are clear that above all else the element of texture is the emphasis for all observations. Interestingly, by relying on emphasis as a principle of design, the instructional leader is allowing for flexibility and creativity on the part of the teachers while also building cohesion around the element of texture within the school.

TENEMENTS: CHICAGO, 1992

Graphite on paper, 12 × 12 in.
Collection of the artist

Principle No. 2

Rhythm: indicates movement by the repetition of elements. The five types are random, regular, alternating, flowing, and progressive.

The Artist's View

Architects often utilize rhythm in constructing buildings, houses, bridges, landscapes, and the like. In some interpretations, the rhythm provides the "heartbeat" of the work. It is the life-giving force or principle. Consider the Golden Gate Bridge in San Francisco. The precise vertical lines create a pattern or "beat" in the visual image. The swooping, plunging cables sustain the life of the vertical cables. In their predictable repetitions, each set of cables offers life-sustaining support to each other, and certainly to the travelers on the road. There is certainty and safety, a sense of permanence, in the use of rhythm.

Rhythm as a Case Study

At the middle school, Ms. Wake is an impressive teacher of students with special needs. In ways in which so many others fail, she can take students with the most challenging behavior problems and make angels out of them. Well, at least for the fifty minutes she teaches them they are angels. As the students arrive from their physical education class, Ms. Wake always has soft music playing in her room. The faint scent of recently burned candles hangs lightly like an early morning mist. The walls are painted with soft images of landscapes and cityscapes. Stars hang randomly across the ceiling. There are green plants and hanging baskets about her room. In the corner of the room there is a loft where students can climb for reading and thinking, or they can go underneath for puzzles. Ms. Wake has an old, white claw-foot tub filled with pillows where students can write in their journals or read storybooks. But most importantly to the students, Ms. Wake's classroom is a place where they are welcomed and embraced. Every day she stops what she is doing as they enter the class and she calls each student by name. Her room is a sanctuary. It has a rhythm of its own. And there, students feel safe.

A Supervision Perspective

Rhythm as a guiding principle for supervision speaks to the patterns of instruction in a class. When an instructional leader tells a teaching staff that the principle of rhythm guides all curriculum and pedagogical decisions, the teachers know that patterns in, or the "heartbeat" of, the class will be the focus. What is it that brings life to the classroom? What distinguishes this room from others? How is this teacher different from others? In seeking the answers to these questions, the instructional leader gains powerful insight into the role that individual personality and creativity play in making for successful lessons.

In many ways, I imagine that rhythm might be one of the most powerful principles. Its power is found in the fact that following its guide forces us to engage the very essence of the lesson. Yes, it is true that the learning outcomes and classroom management need to be addressed. But it is in imagining what gives life to a lesson that the art of supervision is best practiced. Conversely, we have observed lessons where the learning outcomes were met and classroom management supported the attainment of those outcomes but there was no rhythm, no life-giving energy.

For some teachers, the principle of rhythm emerges with the implementation of all elements. In other words, rhythm focuses on the teacher's methods and mannerisms in using the elements of art in instruction. Two second-grade teachers focus on the element of texture in all their lesson planning. They both plan ways to seek out input from all children, drawing on their home cultures to add to the lesson. But the difference in their lessons is dramatic. In one room, the teacher orbits the children and the lesson. In another room, the teacher is part of the lesson and engages the children. Although their lessons are similar in design, their classes have very different rhythms.

I also believe that it is in rhythm that observers may most fully utilize the aesthetic dimension of supervision. When we use Dewey's (1934/1958) view of aesthetic, we come to realize that instructional leadership in matters of rhythm is an attempt to understand the interaction of human beings with their environments. And in that interaction, instructional leaders and teachers draw meaning in reflecting on experience.

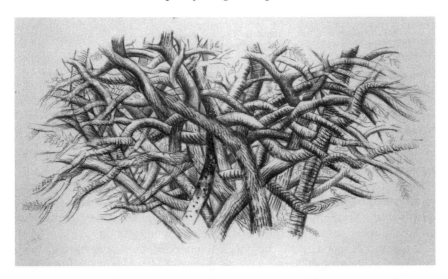

The principle of rhythm, then, demands that everyone in the school ask, "In what ways do I give life to my practices?" and "In what ways do my practices give life to the children and the curriculum?" The answers to questions like these can encourage powerful reflections by all members in the school community. In those reflections we begin to examine the interaction between the teacher, the curriculum, and the students. That reflective experience is the aesthetic of supervision.

DER TIERGARTEN, HERBST NOTIZEN, 1999

Lithograph, 22 × 26 in.
Collection of Cincinnati Art Museum, OH

Principle No. 3

Movement: deals with creating the illusion of action or physical change in position.

The Artist's View

The artist, through the use of line, shape, and color, generates a feeling of turning and moving. The observer might "feel" the wind blowing through a tree as it moves back and forth. Additionally, the lines can lead our eyes from the left side of the painting to the right side, as if carried by the wind. Whereas one might think of a painting in terms of a quiet and still setting, the artist can produce the sensation of movement through the interaction of various elements of art.

Movement as a Case Study

At Monumental High School, the leadership team is considering implementing block scheduling the next school year. The previous summer the assistant principal and two department chairs attended a staff development program that examined alternative scheduling options for large high schools. It is early in the year, and the team imagines that it ought to use the remaining six faculty meetings to introduce and develop the innovation.

At the next faculty meeting, the principal introduces the leadership team and has them explain block scheduling. In that explanation is some discussion about A/B blocking or half-year blocking, about teaching strategies, about learning possibilities. It all seems very exciting. The staff leaves the meeting abuzz with conversation about the innovation. In the few weeks after the introduction of block scheduling, three "camps" of influence begin to emerge.

There are the excited advocates who just cannot see why anyone would question such a clear plan for scheduling. The assistant principal and the two department chairs lead them. At the middle perspective, where the principal sits, is a group of teachers who really do not care what the decision is "just so someone will hurry up and let them know." The principal is interested in producing the least amount of conflict, wherever that leads. At the other extreme is the "it ain't broke and we don't need to fix it" group led by Ms. Polly Permanent and Mr. Tom Tenure, both longtime veterans at the school. They are certain that if they garner enough support from the "undecided vote" they can disrupt yet another innovation and their positions in the school culture will remain unchallenged.

In the next two faculty meetings the two most extreme camps maneuver, cajole, and undercut each other. Allegiances and alliances are the order of the day. Out of three "camps" two sides of the issue emerge. Teachers have to support either the assistant principal and block scheduling or Mr. Tenure and the status quo. The principal announces that everyone has enough information and that at the next faculty meeting he will call for a vote on the issue of block scheduling.

A Supervision Perspective

In matters of supervision and in the matter of the difficult scenario above, the principle of movement guides us to consider several assumptions. First, movement as a principle of design in supervision suggests that we assist teachers and students to move through different levels of knowledge, understanding, and increasingly sophisticated manners of teaching and learning. Second, we begin to address practical questions like, "In what ways do different scheduling plans affect the teachers' movement through the curriculum during the year, a unit, or a lesson?"

If we imagine that movement is the principle of supervision across the school, we begin to look at ways that teachers use the different elements differently in the first of the year versus later in the year. We ask, "Is there a more sophisticated use and understanding of a particular element?" We also might ask, "In what ways are the teachers moving into more complex levels of use within a given element?"

For example, a tenth-grade teacher at the high school is quite good at question-and-answer formats in her government class. She is concerned, however, that her students are growing restless with this single teaching method. She is interested in incorporating some small group work but is frightened of losing control of her class. The instructional supervisor helps the teacher identify and observe different models of small group work, helps her select one that feels right, plans with her how to incorporate it, and then works alongside the teacher in the classroom for the first two attempts to incorporate the new methodology. The leader then allows the teacher to conduct lessons on her own but encourages her to reflect in e-mails to the supervisor on how she thinks the lessons went. As the year progresses, the instructional leader, by providing support and guidance, will continue looking for more advanced and sophisticated use of small-group activity in the teacher's classroom (i.e., movement).

The frightening realization for the instructional leader is that some teachers show no understanding of what movement is as a principle. Everything that they do in December is the same as it was in September. As the instructional leader emphasizing movement as a guiding principle, we are compelled to challenge teachers to reflect on their experience and to find ways to show movement, both on their part and on the part of the students. Doing the same, even when doing the same seems okay, is not acceptable when the guiding principle across the school is movement.

A final example might help round out the comments on movement. If we as instructional leaders are supporting teachers' work trying to incorporate the elements in their lessons, we might find that requiring a standardized program of instruction inhibits their ability to show variety and flexibility. When deciding on a program of study, if we hold to the principle of movement as key to making decisions, we can evaluate that program in light of its support or prevention of movement by individual students and teachers. We might ask, "Does the program allow for differing paces of instruction and learning?" If not, we might consider other programs that do not place a priority on keeping everyone at the same place, on the same pace, thus restricting the potential for individual movement.

KKK (BLACK-BALL), 2001

From the portfolio "Out at Home: Negro Baseball League, Volume II"
Suite of 12 prints, including 3 pages of text, 9 images
Lithograph, 15 × 20 in.
Courtesy, Ellen Sragow Gallery, New York

Principle No. 4

Balance: concerned with equalizing visual forces, or elements.

The Artist's View

By using balance artists can "frame" the object in a painting. An artist
might also use the lack of balance to suggest confusion or frustration. The
viewer might sense tension or that something does not seem to be in order. Similarly, architects might find the use of symmetrical balance important to communicating a sense of stability, safety, and permanence. Or the
architect might use patterns of material or structure to suggest balance or
stability.

Balance as a Case Study

Dr. Lombardi has been principal for four years at one of the district's
eleven elementary schools. He has just entered into his second three-year

contract with the board of education. Dr. Lombardi came to the principal position after ten years as a teacher and football coach at the middle school.

Dr. Lombardi has always enjoyed working hard. He often put in 14-hour days as he tried to balance his work as coach and teacher. In this new job, however, he is surprised to find that at least four days each week he spends 14 hours at school and that weekends are often lost to school responsibilities. During the week, he arrives before 7:00 AM every day, as buses begin arriving at 7:05 AM. After-school responsibilities vary from monitoring the After-School Program to attending open houses, athletic events, plays, musicals, fund-raisers, board meetings, and PTO meetings.

Lately, Dr. Lombardi has found he is quick to lose his temper, often frustrated with the little time he has at home, growing frustrated with parents and teachers, and tired all the time. He is a gifted leader, but he has begun to neglect his own health, both physical and emotional, in the interest of getting the work done at school. Maybe it is time for him to get out of education and enter a work world that is more predictable and less draining.

The school district has instituted a mentoring program for its leadership team, and Dr. Lombardi has been asked to participate. In the process it has become clear to him that his job has taken over his life. If he wants to continue doing what he loves—working with students—he must make some radical changes in his working style. If he does not take back his life, the schoolchildren will lose an important ally, his family life will continue to suffer, and his own health will deteriorate further.

A Supervision Perspective

The principle of balance in matters of supervision is especially important. Balance can speak to many aspects of the instructional leader's life. Like the case study above, it might speak to a balance between personal and professional life. It might speak to maintaining a balance of job responsibilities. A balance in job responsibilities in part demands that the leader reflect on what matters most, on what he/she is spending the most energy and time doing, and the disconnect that might exist between the two. I have found that frustration and burnout often result from not spending the most time doing what we value most. On the contrary, we often spend the most time on the things we value least. The result is a high level of frustration, emotionally and physically. Who of us has not had moments when we wrestled with such challenges? Think of the special education teacher who wants to spend more time with her children but feels that most of her time is spent in IEPs and paperwork. Think of principals who grow weary of the job because they find no time to be in classrooms around children. A colleague of mine worked for years as a biology teacher and then went into administration as an assistant principal, principal, and ultimately a superintendent of schools. He resigned as superintendent because he "was miserable not being around the children." He returned to a high school principal's job, and there were far more children at his retirement ceremony than adults. He was fortunate in that he had recaptured a balance between what he did and what he valued.

I also recognize that balance plays an important role in how an instructional leader can support teacher growth. The most effective action plans for instructional improvement build in appropriate levels of challenge, balanced by appropriate levels of support. Many of us might remember being put into a new job where one felt forced to sink or swim. Sadly, many new teachers face a similarly daunting challenge of sink or swim when they are sent to the classroom with a key and a "good luck." I worked with an art teacher who was new to a school; she was delighted that a mentor was there to support her. The mentor met the teacher the first day and talked about many important matters, such as where to find supplies and how to order materials. At the end of the meeting the mentor remarked, "Let me know if you need any help." The new teacher never saw the mentor again. There was a beginning of support, but in the end there was no support and all challenge.

Instructional leaders do well to create intentional, ongoing, long-range opportunities for support and challenge. When the leadership embraces the notion of balance, teachers relish the challenge of growth in an atmosphere of safety and support. Equally exciting is the fact that when an instructional leader models such a balance, teachers begin to use the same sort of strategies in their classrooms. Balance indeed becomes a principle of design that permeates the school culture.

PORTRAIT OF INNOCENCE, 1993

Lithograph, 12 × 9 in.
Private collection, Vancouver, BC, Canada

Principle No. 5

Proportion: concerned with the size relationships of one part or another.

The Artist's View

Artists recognize that people come in many shapes and sizes but that they generally have the same proportions. Often sculptors capitalize on this notion by placing certain portions of the body out of proportion to what one might normally expect. Take Michelangelo's *David* as an example. The

sculpture is very tall, with head and hands slightly out of proportion to the rest of the body. Although several interpretations might account for this reality, one might conclude that Michelangelo wanted to emphasize the intelligence (e.g., head) and the strength (e.g., hands) as important parts of his message to the viewer. In such ways the artist uses proportion as a tool of expression.

Proportion as a Case Study

The middle school is grappling with reduced funds for the coming year. As a result of the drop in tax revenues in the community, the district did not receive the funds it had anticipated for supporting the approved budget. After much discussion in public meetings, the board of education called for a 3 percent decrease in the next year's budget. The superintendent has notified the middle school principal of the reduction in the operating budget, and now the principal, in the spirit of site-based management, must decide how to adjust.

The middle school prides itself on a wide range of curriculum offerings. In addition to the prescribed courses of study in English, mathematics, social studies, and science, the school also boasts offerings in technology, foreign language, physical education, art, music, home economics, and drama. This variety of offerings has been a luxury, arising in years when the funding was high and the economy solid. Now, things have to change.

One solution that is easy to imagine but painful is to eliminate two of the extra offerings completely (e.g., foreign languages and drama). This choice is painful in part because it eliminates two full-time teachers. Although it is legal, it is rarely easy to release teachers because of funding losses. Reducing the two programs also reduces opportunities for interaction among the increasingly diverse students.

The principal and teachers are unwilling to eliminate the extra offerings. The state department guidelines, however, prevent any reduction in the core academic programs. Given that each of the programs is important to the students and staff, the leadership team sets out to look at the relative costs of each program compared to the cost of operating the overall program. Because of the growing diversity in the student population, the leadership team decides to emphasize one of the foreign languages along with art, reducing them less than the other courses. Foreign languages and art are important to the staff and to the teachers; keeping them as priorities helps sustain the spirit and culture of the institution. Therefore, those two extra offerings remain important in proportion to time and money spent. In the end, the school meets the financial challenge by remembering the role that proportion can play in helping to make decisions that affect all. What was most important received proportionate commitment in the budget.

A Supervision Perspective

Proportion for the instructional supervisor is the guiding principle that helps teachers make decisions about how they spend instructional time. Given the ages, needs, and abilities of the students, effective teachers decide how best to commit time in a class. The instructional leader articulates that when he observes lessons, he wants teachers to explain how proportion is revealed in the lesson and in the unit. At the very least, when teachers begin to think about this explanation they begin to make value and moral judgments about curriculum and instruction. In posing and responding to the question, the instructional leader and teacher alike become aware of the power and responsibility that simple instructional choices can have.

For example, the high school social studies teacher enjoys American history and likes to have students recite the Gettysburg Address. With anywhere between 20 and 25 students in classes, he devotes 7 to 10 days to this task. The instructional leader, though also recognizing the value of the Gettysburg Address, asks the teacher how he can justify spending seven days of instructional time to it. The challenge is not intended to intimidate the teacher into giving up something he clearly thinks is valuable. Rather, the challenge is a specific opportunity for the teacher to explain how his choices are guided by the principle of proportion. When the habit of reflecting on practice and how choices are supported by the guiding principles becomes a habit, teachers understand instruction and curriculum in sophisticated, grounded, and ethical ways.

NIGHT GARDEN, 1994

From the series "Dangerous Gardens"
Charcoal on paper, 50 × 40 in.
Collection of Stephens Investment, Little Rock, AR

Principle No. 6

Variety: concerned with difference or contrast.

The Artist's View

Although a painting can represent a single moment in time, almost a snapshot, the artist may use variety to create many stories at once. For example, the artist

might position individuals in interesting ways so as to suggest "side" conversations amid the larger story. The contrast of individuals, in terms of both shape and color, can capture moments that are at once perplexing and emotional.

Variety as a Case Study

Just recently the district has adopted an assessment instrument for its teachers. Teachers who are in the first, second, or third year of experience are evaluated four times during the school year. Teachers who have more than three years' experience receive evaluations once a year. Additionally, however, the experienced teachers conduct observations of their younger colleagues. Through this type of peer evaluation, the district hopes to capitalize on the many experienced teachers' talents. Also, the district encourages its teachers to collaborate and share effective teaching strategies. The goal of the assessment program is to encourage creative teaching strategies having a common goal of student achievement.

At each faculty meeting, pairs of teachers present some of the successes, challenges, and learning they have garnered by working together. The principal has posted a teaching bulletin board where the stories from the year are collected. By year's end all teaching pairs will have had the opportunity to share their experiences, and the evidence of the variety of teaching strategies will be displayed proudly. The excitement that comes with creative and exploratory energy is growing. Morale is high.

For the most part the program has worked well. Problems are beginning to emerge, however, with certain teachers who are evaluating practice based on their own preferences rather than on objective criteria, such as when students should achieve lesson outcomes. For example, at last month's faculty meeting Mr. Pierson stated that group work is the best strategy for supporting student learning. "Everyone ought to be using cooperative groups!" he proclaims loudly. His less experienced colleague, Ms. Hide, chooses lecture, question-and-answer, and practice work as the best way to help students to learn. She is in her first years of teaching; when asked about group work, she responded, "Group work? I am just trying to survive what I am doing now. I cannot even imagine doing group work with these three preparations I have. Maybe next year I will give it a try." What we have is a classic notion of variety: contrast and difference!

So the principal has two very different teaching strategies presented at the faculty meeting. Both Mr. Pierson and Ms. Hide have successfully completed their evaluations. Student performance for both has been high. The challenge for the principal is to find a way to celebrate the variety of teaching strategies that support high standards without standardizing teaching practice and discouraging creativity.

A Supervision Perspective

Supporting standards without standardizing practice is a significant challenge for instructional supervision. However, when we offer variety as a guiding principle in matters of instruction, the leadership has taken the first steps toward communicating and managing standards as compared to standardization of practice. Variety, while speaking to instructional matters, also may speak to instructional staffs. We might ask, "How does our teaching staff reflect the variety we find in our students in terms of culture and ethnicity?" or "How do our instructional leaders support variety for our teachers?"

In many ways variety as a principle speaks to openness and appreciation. When we work with our teachers, variety as a guide helps remind us to be open to differing viewpoints, to alternative teaching approaches, or maybe to unorthodox concepts of how children learn best. This openness would be bidirectional in nature, as instructional leaders listen to and appreciate teacher ideas and teachers listen to and appreciate leadership ideas. Or, putting it a bit differently, variety would compel us first to come to terms with what another person is doing or saying before we explain our own view or approach.

With such a culture of openness, we could begin asking the difficult question of how differing instructional approaches can meet and exceed standards that we all share. In the case study above, a school culture guided by the principle of variety would go a long way toward resolving the challenges the principal faces. Variety helps us begin talking about alternatives rather than choices. In other words, instead of having to choose either this side or the other side, the teachers and principal could begin finding ways to say this side *and* the other side. Taking votes and choosing sides is not variety. Sharing ideas and finding ways to embrace both sides is more in line with the notion of variety as a principle of design for instructional supervision.

AUTUMN GEISHA, 1999

Acrylic on canvas, 60 × 32 in.
Private collection, River Hills, WI

Principle No. 7

Unity/Harmony: Unity is the quality of wholeness or oneness that is achieved through simplicity, repetition, proximity, and continuation. Harmony creates unity by stressing similarities of separate but related parts.

The Artist's View

What is it about an artwork that makes it feel like it goes together? In what ways do the parts seem to fit? Sometimes it is the sheer act of repeating an element throughout the work that suggests unity. At other times, the artist builds conceptual bridges between separate parts of the work, emphasizing their similarities. Consider music as an example of harmony. When separate but related notes are struck, a harmonic effect emerges. The notes are separate, but the combined sound builds a unity within the work. Visually, a design artist might create wholeness in a clothing line by repeating patterns or colors in a variety of ensembles. Conversely, maybe the lack of decorative designs or multiple colors creates a sense of simplicity that unifies a line of clothing. The visual artist might complete a painting of five individuals in a street scene. They have nothing in common, but by being in the same place at the same time, looking at the same child eating an ice cream, they become joined. They are metaphorically in touch with each other. The artwork, thus, achieves a type of unity or harmony.

Unity/Harmony as a Case Study

It is the first day of school and the principal is rushing to meet the children coming off the bus. The teachers are busy with last-minute classroom preparations. The first big yellow bus arrives, and the children step off into their new world. The shoes are new, the clothes are clean, the backpacks display all the latest toys and cartoon characters. The principal has a call from the central office to meet with a board member. There seems to be a personnel matter with which he must deal. "How can they expect me to be in both places?" he laments. He rushes back to his office, gets his coat, and heads to his car, near where the buses unload their delicate charges. He backs up and heads out, but looking back at the school he notices a child standing at the side of the building, tears rolling down her cheeks. He turns around in the middle of the street and returns to the parking spot.

He approaches the child and asks, "What is wrong?" The child just shuffles and looks down. He then bends to a knee and looks into her eyes and asks, "How can I help you?" The child answers, "I cannot go into school. My father said that since I was old enough to be in school, I was old enough to tie my own shoe. And if I did not, then the other children would make fun of me." The principal, ignoring a second phone call from the central office, reaches down and ties her shoes, takes her by the hand, and helps her to her new room. The principal hands the child to the teacher and says to the child, "Anytime you want help tying your shoes, you come and get me. Together we are going to have a very good year." The phone rings again; the principal starts to answer but instead turns it off and returns to bus duty.

A Supervision Perspective

Harmony/Unity as a principle of supervision commands us to imagine how all that we do in the school to meet standards, address board of education concerns, meet community expectations, and prepare for standardized tests is in line what children need most. Often when we are rushing to complete our lesson plans and to prepare for an upcoming observation, a child seeks us out. When we do not respond to that request or need, there is an inharmonious sound to what we are doing and what we need to be doing.

In a very similar way, when the instructional leader focuses on completing the final three observations before the end of the week but along the way does not respond to the genuine needs of the new teacher in the first observation, that leader has lost a sense of harmony/unity. Instructional supervision is certainly a matter of assessment of teaching performance based on certain expectations. But just as importantly, instructional supervision is also about being aware of personal and professional needs that are not directly or necessarily evident during instruction.

I know that many readers will view my conception of harmony/unity as a principle for supervision as simplistic, unrealistic, or just plain wrong. I have come to believe, however, that even though preparing supervisors to use harmony/unity is a very difficult challenge, it is one we must face. When the harmony/unity is a part of our view, all aspects in a teacher's life can be enhanced. When harmony/unity is a part of instructional supervisors' view, they also benefit from a sense of cohesiveness in their own lives. Although the first beneficiary of such a worldview will be the supervisor, the real beneficiaries will be all the teachers, children, and families with whom he/she comes into contact. Even when there are differences of opinion and some level of discord, harmony/unity will help guide us through the storm that often comes with change and growth.

CONCLUSIONS ON PRINCIPLES OF DESIGN AND THE ART OF SUPERVISION

I have attempted here to describe ways in which the seven principles of design can support supervision. The principles offer us thematic and philosophical guidance as we try to manage the elements of successful supervision. Without the principles' organizing influence, we run the risk of doing lots of important but separate things in our school and thus losing the powerful synergistic effect that principles can offer.

QUESTIONS FOR DISCUSSION

1. Given the seven principles for supervision listed in this chapter, which one(s) do you feel most comfortable with? Why?

2. Which principle of supervision do you lack command of? What might be some specific strategies for developing that principle?
3. Identify one principle that you believe would be useful for many leaders and design a staff development program for your school where you could introduce and develop that principle.
4. Reflect on current realities at your school setting and identify one problem as an area for growth. Develop an action plan that uses one or more of the principles to facilitate your school's effort to address that problem. In your action plan, remember to identify a specific goal, some potential obstacles, a timetable, and an assessment for determining your level of success.
5. Which principle holds the greatest promise for you personally and professionally? How can you develop that principle more fully? How can you monitor your own growth?
6. Select one of the case studies and apply the "Art of Leadership Critique." Remember to describe what happened, analyze particular behaviors, find meaning, and evaluate the leadership.

Art of Leadership Critique
Topic/Issue at Hand: _____
Leader Name: _____
School/System Setting: _____
Date: _____

Step 1: Description
The goal is to describe objectively what you see; to delay judgment. List system, leader, date; describe setting and key players; identify central or core issue; identify elements of leadership that are present.
A description might include: _____ __

_____

_____

Step 2: Analysis
The goal is to describe behaviors of what you see. Describe how the elements listed in step 1 use the principles of leadership. Which principles provide organization for the elements? List your emotional reaction to these factors. How does the leadership strategy make you feel? How does it make others feel?
The analysis might include: _____

_____

_____

Step 3: Interpretation

The goal is to find meaning in what you see. Does it work? Why? What do you think the leader is trying to do? What is the goal? What are the symbolic goals that emerge? What do they mean?

One interpretation might be:_____

_____

_____

Step 4: Judgment

The goal is to evaluate what you see. How could the leader have been more successful? Who benefits from the decisions? Who does not? What balance is there between what the leader says, what he does, and what he believes? What is the relationship between what the school values, believes, and does?

A possible judgment would include: _____

_____

_____

9

The Art of Supervision:
An Overview

In working with the elements of art and the principles of design in matters of supervision, I am working from the assumption that there is indeed an aesthetic dimension in supervision. Many of the researchers outlined in chapter 6 have crafted powerful and meaningful theoretical frameworks for assisting teachers to help students achieve, but they have not in specific ways seen supervision as art. Even Blumberg's work stopped short of thinking of supervision as art; he imagined it more in terms of craft. But I do imagine and hope that my contribution to the supervision conversation enlarges, extends, and maybe even challenges current modes of supervision.

At the outset of this discussion on supervision as art, I acknowledged that there has been some confusion about what exactly supervision was and how it might best be defined. I have come to believe, through my readings, interviews, and my own professional experiences that the difficulty of definition lies in the fact that we are reluctant to acknowledge that teaching, when done well, is art, and thus that supervision of teaching, when done well, must also be art. But if supervision is art, we will have to consider our preparation and training programs wholly insufficient. Buying into that realization is potentially threatening at the very least, because it would challenge each of us, administrators and professors alike, to change our modus operandi.

Defining and delineating the art of teaching is elusive and tricky. Many of the characteristics of teaching done well, or what I called in an earlier chapter "criterial attributes," are more aesthetic than technical in nature. Think of the effective teacher who creates an inviting and safe learning space for children; compare that teacher to another who uses many of the same skills but creates an environment that children dread and fear. Much of the difference is not the technical, the clinical, or the observable. The differences are found in the more subtle choreography of human interaction. Consider how the artist teacher greets students, the nonverbal cues and feedback she offers, her movement through the lesson and through the period, and her creation of a "set" in the classroom. For the artistic teacher, the classroom is a stage. For the purely technical teacher, the classroom is a loading dock. She has something the students need—the answers to her test. The students arrive at her classroom, she deposits the skills and knowledge, and then they move on to the next loading station (i.e., classroom or lesson).

The artistic teacher, on the other hand, has a plan for instruction as well. And she will want students to carry away important information that will, she hopes, help the students perform well on standardized tests. But performance on standardized assessments is not sufficient. She knows that students do well when they have command of content knowledge. She knows that students achieve when she teaches well. But just as importantly, she recognizes the power of human interaction in supporting student achievement. When students develop strong relationships with their teachers and with their peers, they are more likely to have academic success. It is in this last notion that the artistic teacher most notably distinguishes herself from the technical instructor. On the stage that is her classroom, the students and teacher will move toward a goal, but there will be no exact, preordained path. Rather, the teacher and students will engage in a dance of understanding, where they respond to her lead and move across the floor to a place characterized by a more profound level of connection with the subject matter, with each other, and with themselves. For the artistic teacher and her students, the choreography of the learning process is as important and valuable as the learning product.

Given the nature of the teaching as art, supervision of teaching can similarly escape definition when it takes on its most powerful manifestation— that is to say, when it becomes an aesthetic process. Let us consider three broad themes that are requisite for an instructional leader to become an artist of his/her craft.

First, if supervision is about data collection and inspection, we can manage those tasks, those ends, with specificity and concrete measures. But when supervision becomes a process whereby the instructional supervisor and teacher discuss the possible meaning and value of the lesson, we elevate conversation to a very different level of analysis. It is in this notion of interaction that supervision becomes aesthetic in nature. Through conversation, the supervisor becomes critic, in the sense of artistic criticism, and the teacher becomes artist, describing and explaining the product of his/her labor. Barone (1988), in clarifying Eisner's view of educational criticism, states, "Educational connoisseurship is the art of appreciating educational phenomena. Educational criticism, then, is the art of disclosing what it is that has come to be appreciated. Connoisseurship, therefore, is a prerequisite to criticism" (p. 1115).

What this means for supervision as art is that, first, to be an instructional leader with a view of the art of teaching one must have lived, worked, and studied in ways that prepare one to become an artistic teacher. In other words, one must be a connoisseur of the art of teaching. Then and only then can one begin to view teaching from an artistic perspective and thereafter offer criticism about what is to be discussed and appreciated. At the most basic level, this understanding requires that instructional leaders return regularly and often to the classroom so that they can retain and develop their own art. A colleague of mine is an art teacher and offers art classes to children in the summer. She has often remarked that she must make time for her own art, that she will lose the sharpness of her craft if all she does is teach others. The same seems to go for instructional leaders—and, I might add, professors of instruction. They too must return regularly to the classrooms in order to retain the feel for what teaching is, to remain a connoisseur of the art.

Second, I also note in my supervision-as-art premise that the key to the aesthetics or the conversations between the instructional leader and the teacher is the art of conversation itself. Most importantly, I speak of the notion of empathic conversation and understanding. Instructional supervisors can observe many things in a class. Many of our objective concerns are with the measurable and observable outcomes of a lesson; I suggest that many people can be trained as data collectors. But it is a different story when the instructional leader not only observes what can be counted and measured but "sees" the emotion, the rhythm, and the art in the lesson. Empathic understanding, then, is a necessary talent if one is to begin to see supervision as an art form. The supervisor who can view a lesson with empathy can recreate the emotion and the feelings of the teacher and the students. The leader must not only see what is going on but feel the ebb and flow of energy, of anxieties, or of confidences. It is as if the instructional supervisor has an electrocardiogram of the lesson and upon reflection can sense when the "beat" of the lesson quickens and when it slows. A supervisor can learn these skills only through the intentional and ongoing practice of empathic listening, thus becoming a connoisseur of the art of conversation.

Thus far I have argued that supervision, as art, requires one to be a connoisseur of teaching as well as to be in command of the art of empathic understanding. The third leg on which supervision as art stands is the art of stories and critiques. Simply put, if we continue to evaluate teaching using traditional or standardized checklists, our instrument will reduce the experience to inspection no matter how hard we try to view teaching as art. Thus, from the supervisor-as-artist perspective, an appropriate assessment instrument might be the best construction of a story. The lesson has actors, a lead player, supporting roles, underlying themes, plots and subplots, all the makings of a good mystery or drama. One way instructional leaders might construct a narrative of what is seen is to follow a pattern similar to Feldman's criticism: describe, analyze, interpret, and judge. However, the key to this notion of storytelling is remembering that narrative (from the Latin word *narrare*) is in relating events and the way those events interact with each other and add meaning to experience.

All this discussion about criticism, aesthetics, connoisseurship, empathic understanding, and narrative storytelling leads me exactly to the point where I can close with comments on the purposes of the elements of art and the principles of design and how they inform instructional practice. But I am certain that one's capacity to use the elements and principles effectively is related to one's command over and facility with the three themes of connoisseurship, empathic understanding, and narrative storytelling discussed above.

The elements of art offer instructional leaders specific methodologies for seeing supervision more as art and craft than as inspection and evaluation. The elements (line, shape, form, space, color, value, and texture) are specific and most often used by instructional leaders with specific teachers or for specific purposes. The elements are more readily undertaken by novices in the field of supervision precisely because of their specificity. In one school, an instructional leader can work with one element for all teachers or several elements for several different teachers. The decision is tied up in the process of developing lesson and unit plans and what an emphasis might be for a particular lesson or teacher.

The principles of design (emphasis, rhythm, movement, balance, proportion, variety, harmony/unity) offer instructional leaders more thematic, philosophical, and guiding methodologies for seeing supervision as art. Although the elements tend to be specific and concrete, the principles are often broad and abstract. But the value of the principles, in part, is that they offer unifying themes that transcend entire schools or even districts. This idea was more fully developed earlier in this book, but it is worth noting again that in joining a group of teachers through principles we do not restrict them to single methodologies and perspectives. Herein lies the beauty of the principles. Their use embraces teachers under themes but also encourages individual interpretation and application of how those themes might be manifested in the specific classrooms or in specific elements.

The elements of art and principles of design then offer us a mechanism to discuss, describe, evaluate, and listen to what teaching and learning look and feel like when conducted as an art form.

QUESTIONS FOR DISCUSSION

1. In what ways might teaching be characterized as technical or scientific?
2. In what ways does teaching take on an artistic dimension?
3. In what circumstances might supervision be best practiced as a technical skill?
4. In what settings might supervision be best practiced as art?
5. Compare and contrast supervision as art versus supervision as scientific.
6. Offer your philosophy of supervision. In what ways might you see yourself as an artist? In what ways are you a technician?

10

Leadership and Supervision as Art: What I Have Learned

In undertaking this examination, I imagined that I could construct a mechanism for observing school leadership and instructional supervision that might broaden my view, deepen my understanding, and sharpen my insight into what makes for successful schools. I have risked much by trying to link the two worlds, leadership and art, and many will remain skeptical or unconvinced after reading my work. As a mentor of mine, Professor Ray Bruce, warned: "The farther away from the day to day workings of school you are, the better such an approach might appear." Clearly, he was suspicious that my work might be neither practical nor realistic. I hope that my work with school leaders and instructional supervisors has kept me grounded in the real world of schooling. They too were at first skeptical because the link between art and leadership was not obvious. But as we worked together to better understand the art of the practice, we began to see the connection of applying the language of art criticism to the practice of school leadership and instructional supervision. It was not easy, but then again, most effective leadership in schools, or elsewhere, cannot be done well without considerable effort. Through it all, I want to offer insights into what I have found. In applying the elements of art and the principles of design to leadership and to supervision, I found that some views were similar and others were very dissimilar. Sometimes, the view was the very much the same, because supervision is often a component of the larger view of school leadership. But at other times, the application of the elements and principles brought a different perspective to leadership as art versus supervision as art. Below, I offer some encapsulating summaries of what I have learned. With each element or principle I offer a word and then a very brief statement that seems to capture the essence of the message. Likewise, I have placed leadership as art and supervision as art in juxtaposition with each element or principle so as to allow for comparison.

With regard to elements of art as constructs for leadership and supervision:

Leadership as Art:	Limits. Be clear about boundaries and parameter. Communicate expectations.
Supervision as Art:	Expectations. What are the limits? Boundaries? What might I expect from this relationship?

Value

Leadership as Art:	Priority. Decide what matters most, devote your energy there, do the other things as necessary or as time allows.
Supervision as Art:	Priority. How can I help the teacher reflect on what is pressing, what is important?

Shape

Leadership as Art:	Management. Do what needs to be done so that you can do what ought to be done.
Supervision as Art:	Details. What am I doing to help the teacher see all the noninstructional challenges that affect performance?

Form

Leadership as Art:	Perspective. Can I "see" what you are seeing? How do things appear from your point of reference?
Supervision as Art:	Empathy. Can I discern what the teacher is saying, not saying, means to say?

Space

Leadership as Art:	Collaboration. Find ways to support and to challenge. Balance the two. Long-term collaboration offers support amid challenges.
Supervision as Art:	Growth. What can a teacher manage? What is too much? The proper balance creates opportunities for growth.

Color

Leadership as Art:	Differences/Similarities. How can I invite diversity of ideas? Am I celebrating different paths, journeys?
Supervision as Art:	Diversity. How can I support standards for instruction but also embrace diverse teaching styles?

Texture

Leadership as Art:	Tapestry. In what ways have I invited participation by stakeholders? Has anyone been marginalized?
Supervision as Art:	Bridges. How can we bring staff together in meaningful partnerships?

With regard to principles of design as constructs for leadership and supervision:

Emphasis

Leadership as Art:	Headlines. How do we see ourselves? How do we want others to see us? What are first impressions?
Supervision as Art:	Focus. Given the diversity of teaching styles, what will be our schoolwide focus for improving instruction?

Rhythm

Leadership as Art:	Flow. How do our decisions support priorities? Are we in step with the music?
Supervision as Art:	Heartbeat. In what ways can I identify and support the creative elements in a lesson that bring it to life?

Movement

Leadership as Art:	Progress. Are we productive or are we just busy? Do we work hard or smart?
Supervision as Art:	Developmental. In what ways is instruction growing in sophistication; in variability?

Balance

Leadership as Art:	Stability. Is my personal life supporting my professional life? Or is my personal life a casualty of my work?
Supervision as Art:	Bidirectionality. In what ways am I supporting teacher growth and my own professional growth? Am I kindling my own fire?

Proportion

Leadership as Art:	Relationship. Does our use of time and energy follow our priority? How are they connected?

Supervision as Art: Prescription. In what ways are the teacher's choices
                     an appropriate plan for the needs and abilities of the
                     students?

Variety

Leadership as Art: Multiplicity. So many ways to get there! Are we al-
                     lowing for individual creativity amid shared commit-
                     ments?
Supervision as Art: Creativity. While demanding standards, how can we
                     also support individual creativity and not standardi-
                     zation of practice?

Harmony/Unity

Leadership as Art: Presence. Am I present with my students, teachers,
                     family, self?
Supervision as Art: Connections. In what ways can we remain in touch
                     with what children need when so many external
                     matters confront us?

In my listing above I have attempted to encapsulate some of my learning and
my message into a simple format. Necessarily, I have lost depth by presenting
such a visual. But I have also found the exercise helpful to begin coming to
terms with leadership as art and supervision as art. Not surprisingly, rather than
differences in substances or type, supervision and leadership both emerge from
a common set of assumptions about human motivation and interaction. And as
such, an examination of leadership and supervision begins to be more about
subtle differences on a single continuum rather than about extreme contrasts or
"either or" conclusions about their natures. And in my view, that continuum informs us that leadership and supervision are about relationships that we create
and cultivate. It is in the qualitative nature of relationships that the choreography of human understanding begins to take form and leadership becomes art.

Afterword

I so much enjoy visiting a museum and watching people view an artwork. They approach it and stop. Then they move away from it, they move close to it, over and over, back and forth. I think of it as a type of "dance of understanding." Much as a work of art has one appearance from a distance and a different one up close, effective leadership and supervision call for a type of choreography of human understanding. And in that dance with each other among the important, and sometimes not so important, matters of the school day, we elevate each other to higher levels of performance, higher levels of existence.

From a desk in a graduate school classroom, leadership and supervision can appear simple and formulaic. But as we walk down the halls of schools and view teachers and leaders in their most basic, authentic, and familiar aspects, we begin to see elements and principles that individually and collectively help educators create places of learning and caring. I suggest that as we begin to understand the concept of leadership and supervision, as well as the ambiguities created by different people at different places and times, we can provide some room for creative construction of modes of leadership and supervision based on those same variables. But this is not to say that leadership and supervision have no constructs or that I am suggesting practice without substance or rigor. Rather, by applying to effective leadership and supervision our understanding of the seven elements and seven principles, maybe we can support our school leaders and teachers with important standards of leadership without standardizing the art that is leadership.

Leadership and instructional supervision are not the responsibility of the leader alone, any more than the art is the function of only one element or principle. Rather, it is the interplay of people's strengths and weaknesses that makes schools good or bad. It is the artistic leader who brings together those multiple threads of human existence to construct a tapestry characterized by learning, teaching, and children. And it is this delicate dance of human understanding that makes leading in schools so daunting and so very exciting. May we have the courage to take the first step.

Appendix A

Art of Leadership Critique

Topic/Issue at Hand:_____

Leader Name:_____

School/System Setting:_____

Date:_____

Step 1: Description

The goal is to describe objectively what you see; to delay judgment. List system, leader, date; describe setting and key players; identify central or core issue; identify elements of leadership that are present.

A description might include: _____

_____

_____

Step 2: Analysis

The goal is to describe behaviors of what you see. Describe how the elements listed in step 1 use the principles of leadership. Which principles provide organization for the elements? List your emotional reaction to these factors. How does the leadership strategy make you feel? How does it make others feel?

The analysis might include: _____

_____

_____

Step 3: Interpretation
The goal is to find meaning in what you see. Does it work? Why? What do you think the leader is trying to do? What is the goal? What are the symbolic goals that emerge? What do they mean?
One interpretation might be: _____

_____

_____

Step 4: Judgment
The goal is to evaluate what you see. How could the leader have been more successful? Who benefits from the decisions? Who does not? What balance is there between what the leader says, what he does, and what he believes? What is the relationship between what the school values, believes, and does?
A possible judgment would include: _____

_____

_____

Appendix B

Action Plan to Strengthen Leadership and Supervision Elements

Leader's Name:_____

Mentor's Name:_____

Cycle: 1 2 3_____

Date:_____

List Leadership/Supervision Elements with which I am comfortable: ____

_____

_____

_____

List one Leadership/Supervision Element on which to focus: _____

_____

_____

_____

Plan of Action:

1. Read and/or review the following: _____

_____

_____

_____

2. Observe another using the leadership/supervision element: _____

_____

_____

_____

3. Practice the element in the following ways: _____

_____

_____

_____

4. Demonstrate successful understanding of the element by: _____

_____

_____

_____

Time needed: _____

_____

_____

_____

Resources needed (workshops, personnel, materials, reading, video-
tapes, etc.): _____

_____

_____

_____

Appendix C

Action Plan to Strengthen Leadership and Supervision Principles

Leader's Name:_____

Mentor's Name:_____

Cycle: 1 2 3_____

Date:_____

List Leadership/Supervision Principles with which I am comfortable: _____

_____

_____

_____

List one Leadership/Supervision Principle on which to focus: _____

_____

_____

_____

Plan of Action:

1. Read and/or review the following:_____

_____

_____

_____

2. Observe another using the leadership/supervision principle: _____

_____

_____

_____

3. Practice the principle in the following ways: _____

_____

_____

_____

4. Demonstrate successful understanding of the principle by: _____

_____

_____

_____

Time needed: _____

_____

_____

_____

Resources needed (workshops, personnel, materials, reading, video-tapes, etc.): _____

_____

_____

Appendix D

New Leadership Skill Readiness Self-Assessment

AM I READY FOR DEVELOPING LEADERSHIP AND SUPERVISION SKILLS AS AN ART FORM?

Part 1

Place a check by any feelings you have experienced in the last two weeks. These feelings can take place at any location (i.e., home, work, church, play).

- Going from positive to negative feelings rapidly
- Losing or misplacing things
- Exhaustion
- Short temper
- Defensive behavior
- Extremely critical or judgmental statements
- Propensity toward accidents

0–1 check   = 10 points
2–3 checks = 20 points
4–5 checks = 35 points
6–7 checks = 50 points

Part 1 total _____

Part 2

In the last 20 to 30 days, how would you characterize your preferred leadership style?

Category A

- I enjoy specific and concrete assignments; I prefer highly structured activities
- I enjoy pleasing others
- I tend to be very uncomfortable with ambiguity
- When I listen to others I find it difficult to recognize their feelings.

Category B

- I prefer a mix of specific/concrete and abstract assignments
- I prefer some absolutes in life
- I enjoy some structure but like to take risks sometimes
- Sometimes I can tell what others are feeling when I listen to them.

Category C

- I view knowledge as a process of successive approximations
- I find that absolutes in life make me uncomfortable; ambiguity is okay
- I find structure uncomfortable and restrictive; I prefer risk-taking
- I easily recognize feelings in others during conversations.

If you are Category A, then you get 50 points.
If you are Category B, then you get 25 points.
If you are Category C, then you get 10 points.

Part 2 total _____

Part 3

When you think about developing elements of art for leadership or principles of design for leadership, your first question is:

1. Do I really want to do this?
2. Where do I begin?
3. How is this going to help me with my job?
4. How can I manage this with everything else I am doing?
5. How will doing this help my coworkers or my students?
6. Is there anyone I can work with who would be interested in the same sort of development?

If your question was most like numbers 1 or 2, you get 50 points.
If your question was most like numbers 3 or 4, you get 25 points.
If your question was most like numbers 4, 5, or 6, you get 10 points.

Part 3 total _____

Summary Assessment

Category	Points
Part 1 (levels of stress)	_____
Part 2 (current preferred leadership style)	_____
Part 3 (stage of concern)	_____
Total	_____

If you scored between:

1. 30–40, then your stress is reasonably low and your chances for success when taking on this new dimension are good.
2. 40–50, then your stress is moderately elevated and you will need go slowly and be patient with the process of this new dimension.
3. 50–75, then your stress is elevated and the competing demands in your life, whether at home or at work, reduce your likelihood of success.
4. Above 75, then your stress is high and taking on new challenges will be especially tough as you try to manage the competing demands in your life. Additionally, there may exist a "disconnect" between what you value and what you do.

The guidelines above are just that—guidelines. Each person should reflect on his/her own experiences to determine how he/she feels about taking on new challenges. The message: We should be fair and sensible with ourselves in considering what we can reasonably take on and what might best be left to another time or another person.

© Zach Kelehear

Appendix E

Active Listening Analysis Form

Directions for this page: Tape-record a conversation with a family member, colleague, or student. At a private and quiet time, listen to your conversation with the chart below at hand. As you analyze the tape of your conversation or conference, write under "Active Listening Behaviors" the comments you made that show a particular category of active listening (direct quotes or close paraphrases). In the other column, make a note of "Missed Opportunities"—those occasions where you could have given an active listening response but didn't.

	Active Listening Behaviors	Missed Opportunities
Level 1: Paraphrase Feelings		
Level 2: Paraphrase Content		
Level 3: Door Openers ("Tell me more.") Acknowledgments ("Sure." "Right." "Uh huh." "Yes.")		

Directions for this section: As you analyze the tape of your conversation or
conference, write under "Nonlistening Behaviors" the comments you made
that show a particular category of "nonlistening" (direct quotes or close paraphrases). In the other column, make a note of what you could have said instead in order to provide an active listening response. (Sometimes the best
substitute may be "silence.")

	Nonlistening Behaviors	Do/say instead?
Level 4: Roadblocks (Label each example.)*		
Level 5: Hooking statements (Using the other's words to "hook" them into your conversation.)		
Level 6: Ships passing in the night (Parallel conversations, having little or nothing to do with each other.)		

*Roadblocks are those responses that stop the other person from pursuing
his/her own train of thought and feelings and cause him/her to stop talking
or to go in your direction. Roadblocks commonly take one of the following
forms: directing, ordering, warning, threatening, moralizing, preaching, per-
suading, arguing, advising, recommending, evaluating, criticizing, question-
ing, probing, praising, supporting, sympathizing, diagnosing, diverting, by-
passing, kidding, teasing, or hanging on to a pet idea.

OVERALL REFLECTION ON YOUR ACTIVE LISTENING SKILLS

1. What were the two main levels of your listening (or nonlistening) responses? _____

   _____

   _____

2. Becoming a good active listener means increasing your active listening behaviors (levels 1–3) and decreasing, or eliminating, the roadblocks and other nonlistening responses (levels 4–6). In what ways have you improved since your last analysis? In what ways would you still like to improve? _____

_____

_____

3. Reflect further on your listening skills in this space or on additional paper:_____

_____

_____

_____

References

Acheson, K. A., & Gall, M. D. (1980). *Techniques in the clinical supervision of teachers*. White Plains, NY: Longman.

Anderson, L. W., & Krathwohl, D. R. (Eds.). (2001). *A taxonomy for learning, teaching, and assessing: A revision of Bloom's taxonomy of educational objectives*. New York: Longman.

Barone, T. E. (1998). Aesthetic dimensions of supervision. In G. R. Firth & E. F. Pajak (Eds.), *Handbook of research on school supervision* (pp. 1104–1122). New York: Simon & Schuster Macmillan.

Bennis, W., & Nanus, B. (1997). *Leaders: Strategies for taking charge* (2nd ed.). New York: HarperBusiness.

Bolin, F. (1987). Perspectives and imperatives: On defining supervision. *Journal of curriculum and supervision, 2* (4), pp. 368–380.

Bolman, L. G., & Deal, T. E. (1995). *Leading with soul: An uncommon journey of spirit*. San Francisco: Jossey-Bass.

Blumberg, A. (1974). *Supervisors and teachers: A private cold war*. Berkeley, CA: McCutchan.

Blumberg, A. (1989). *School administration as a craft: Foundations of practice*. Boston: Allyn & Bacon.

Buckingham, M., & Coffman, C. (1999). *First, break all the rules: What the world's greatest managers do differently*. New York: Simon & Schuster.

Cogan, M. L. (1973). *Clinical supervision*. Boston: Houghton Mifflin.

Conner, D. R. (1992). *Managing at the speed of change*. New York: Villard Books.

Costa, A. L., & Garmston, R. J. (1994). *Cognitive coaching: A foundation for renaissance schools*. Norwood, MA: Christopher-Gordon.

Covey, S. R. (1989). *The seven habits of highly effective people*. New York: Simon & Schuster.

Dewey, J. (1934/1958). *Art as experience*. New York: Capricorn Books.

Dow, A. W. (1899). *Composition: A series of exercises selected from a new system of art education.* Boston: J. M. Bowles.

Dow, A. W. (1997). *Composition: A series of exercises in art structure for the use of students and teachers.* Berkeley: University of California Press.

Eisner, E. W. (1982). An artistic approach to supervision. In T. J. Sergiovanni (Ed.).*Supervision of teaching* (1982 Yearbook) pp. 35–52. Alexandria, VA: ASCD.

Eisner, E. W. (1983). The art and craft of teaching. *Educational Leadership, 40* (4).

Eisner, E. W. (1985). *The educational imagination: On the design and evaluation of school programs* (2nd ed.). New York: Macmillan.

Eisner, E. W. (1997). *Educating artistic vision.* New York: Macmillan.

Eisner, E. W. (2002). *The arts and the creation of mind.* New Haven: Yale University Press.

Eye, G. G. & Netzer, L. A. (1965). *Supervision of instruction: A phase of administration.* New York: Harper & Row.

Feldman, E. B. (1995). Philosophy of art education. New Jersey: Prentice Hall.

Fish, S. (2004). Minimalism. *The Chronicle of Higher Education, 50* (42), C1, C4.

Fuller, F. (1969). Concerns of teachers: A developmental conceptualization. *American Educational Research Journal, 6* (2), 207–226.

Gardner, J. W. (1990). *On leadership.* New York: Free Press.

Garman, N. B. (1986). Reflection, the heart of clinical supervision: A modern rationale for practice. *Journal of Curriculum and Supervision, 2* (1), 1–24.

Glanz, J. (1998). Histories, antecedents, and legacies of school supervision. In G. R. Firth & E. F. Pajak (Eds.), *Handbook of research on school supervision* (pp. 39–79). New York: Simon & Schuster Macmillan.

Glickman, C. (2002). *Leadership for learning: How to help teachers succeed.* Alexandria, VA: Association for Supervision and Curriculum Development.

Glickman, C. D., Gordon, S. P., & Ross-Gordon, J. M. (2004). *SuperVision and instructional leadership: A developmental approach.* Boston: Allyn & Bacon.

Goldhammer, R. (1969). *Clinical supervision: Special methods for the supervision of teachers.* New York: Holt, Rinehart & Winston.

Gordon, S. P. (1997). Has the field of supervision evolved to a point that it should be called something else? Yes. In J. Glanz and R. F. Neville (Eds.), *Educational supervision: Perspectives, issues, and controversies*, pp. 114–123. Norwood, MA: Christopher-Gordon.

Greene, M. (1995). *Releasing the imagination.* San Francisco: Jossey-Bass.

Greene, M. (2001). *Variations on a blue guitar.* New York: Teachers College Press.

Harris, B. M. (1998). Paradigms and parameters of supervision in education. In G. R. Firth & E. F. Pajak (Eds.), *Handbook of research on school supervision* (pp. 1–37). New York: Simon & Schuster Macmillan.

Howard, V. (1982). *Artistry: The work of artists.* Indianapolis, MN: Hackett.

Hunter, M. (1984). Knowing, teaching, and supervising. In P. L. Hofford (Ed.), *Using what we know about teaching.* Alexandria, VA: ASCD.

Jackson, P. W. (1998). *John Dewey and the lessons of art.* New Haven, CT: Yale University Press.

Kelehear, Z. (2002, Fall). Tell me what went well with your lesson, Sam: E-mail with empathy helps new teachers to grow. *Journal of Staff Development, 23* (4), 33–36.

Kelehear, Z. (2001, Fall). Empathic writing as a function of effective leadership: E-mail and the principal as leader. *American Association of Behavioral and Social Sciences Journal*, 39–46.

Kouzes, J. M., & Posner, B. Z. (1995). *The leadership challenge: How to keep getting extraordinary things done in organizations* (2nd ed.). San Francisco: Jossey-Bass.

Lambert, L. (2003). *Leadership capacity for lasting school improvement.* Alexandria, VA: Association for Curriculum and Curriculum Development.

Lawrence-Lightfoot, S. (1983). *The good high school: Portraits of character and culture.* New York: Basic Books.

Lawrence-Lightfoot, S., & Davis, J. H. (1997). *The art and science of portraiture.* San Francisco: Jossey-Bass.

Lewis, A. C. (2004, March). Schools that engage children. *Phi Delta Kappan, 85* (7), 483.

Martorella, P. H. (1985). *Elementary social studies: Developing reflective, competent, and concerned citizens.* Boston: Little, Brown.

Maxwell, J. C. (1998). *The 21 irrefutable laws of leadership: Follow them and people will follow you.* Nashville, TN: Thomas Nelson.

Maxwell, J. C. (2002). *Leadership 101.* Nashville, TN: Thomas Nelson.

Oliva, P. F., & Pawlas, G. E. (2004). *Supervision for today's schools.* Hoboken, NJ: Wiley.

Pajak, E. (2000). *Approaches to clinical supervision: Alternatives for improving instruction* (2nd ed.). Norwood, MA: Christopher-Gordon.

Pajak, E. (2003). *Honoring diverse teaching styles: A guide for supervisors.* Alexandria, VA: Association for Supervision and Curriculum Development.

Patterson, J. (1998, March). Harsh realities about decentralized decision making. *The School Administrator, 55* (3), 6–10, 12.

Ragans, R. (1995). *Art talk.* Boston: Glencoe/McGraw-Hill.

Sergiovanni, T. J. (2000). Leadership as stewardship: "Who's serving who?" In *The Jossey-Bass reader on educational leadership.* San Francisco: Jossey-Bass.

Sergiovanni, T. J., & Starratt, R. J. (2002). *Supervision: A redefinition* (7th ed.). Boston: McGraw-Hill.

Smyth, J. W. (1985, January–March). *Developing a critical practice of clinical supervision. Journal of Curriculum and Supervision, 17,* 1–15.

Starratt, R. J. (2003). *Centering educational administration: Cultivating meaning, community, and responsibility.* Mahwah, NJ: Lawrence Erlbaum.

Starratt, R. J. (2004). *Ethical leadership.* San Francisco: Jossey-Bass.

Steinbeck, J. (1955, November). . . . Like captured fireflies. *California Teachers Association Journal, 51* (8), 7.

Taylor, P. (Ed). (2002). *Amazing grace: The lithographs of Joseph Norman.* Boston: Museum of the National Center of Afro-American Artists.

Waite, D. (1995). *Rethinking instructional supervision: Notes on its language and culture.* Washington, DC: Falmer.

Zeichner, K. M., & Liston, D. P. (1996). *Reflective teaching: An introduction.* Mahwah, NJ: Lawrence Erlbaum.

Index

active listening, 31, 81–82, 87–88,
141–43
aesthetics, vii–xii, 1–3, 7–8, 71–72,
73–76, 104–5, 121–24
arts-based research, xii–xiv, 70
Art Talk, xii, 1
Assessing Developing Evaluating
Performances in Teaching (ADEPT),
68
assessment, 68, 39, 56, 67–68, 72, 87–88,
123; standardized, 43, 101, 107, 114,
118, 122–23
attributes, 1, 7, 9, 44, 62, 68; criterial vs.
noncriterial, 10–12, 20, 121
authentic, x–xi, xiv, 3, 11, 19, 59, 79,
129

balance. *See* principles of design
Bloom's Taxonomy, 3

change, 14, 17, 21, 36, 38, 47, 51, 53,
118, 121
color. *See* elements of art
communication, x, xii, xiii, 43, 65, 126;
effective, 12–13, 31, 84–88, 86–90;
interpersonal, 12, 20, 46; nonverbal,
31, 44, 49–50, 77–81, 87, 101, 109,
122
connoisseur, 122–24

core values, x, xiii, 9–10, 14, 26, 39, 99
criticism, 2–3, 122–25
culture, 11–12, 36, 44, 48–49, 54, 93, 95,
104–6, 110–12, 115
curriculum, x, 43–44, 53, 71, 78, 92–93,
99–105, 112–14

dance, xi, 1, 3, 5, 96, 122
decision making, viii, xiii, 2–3, 6–7,
9–10, 16, 18, 41, 44, 46, 48–49,
52–54, 64, 77–78, 91, 99, 102–7, 112,
127
differentiation, 56–57, 93–95, 104–7, 126
diversity, 36–38, 53–54, 63, 68–70,
93–95, 102, 112, 126–27

effective communication. *See*
communication, effective
effective schools, xiv, 21
effective teaching, xiv, 56, 71, 90, 96,
112–14, 121
e-mail. *See* communication
emphasis. *See* principles of design
elements of art: color, xii–xiii, 5, 7, 21,
34–36, 73, 91, 93, 96, 124–26; form,
xii–xiii, 5–7, 21–22, 30–31, 33–34,
36, 63, 73, 86–88, 96, 124, 126; line,
xii–xiii, 6–7, 21–25, 38, 63, 73,
76–79, 96, 124, 126; shape, xii–xiii,

About the Author

Dr. Zach Kelehear is an associate professor of educational leadership at the University of South Carolina in Columbia. Before joining USC, he taught at the University of Alabama at Birmingham. Kelehear teaches graduate-level courses in leadership and instructional supervision. He previously served as Director of Personnel and Staff Development for Dalton Public Schools in Dalton, Georgia. He has also taught undergraduate and graduate courses in Education at Furman University in Greenville, South Carolina, where he received the prestigious Meritorious Teaching Award in his third year at that highly selective liberal arts institution. Having pursued a double major of Latin and history, Kelehear taught those subjects in grades eight through twelve in DeKalb County Schools in suburban Atlanta, Georgia. Kelehear also consults with schools, churches, and businesses in the areas of leadership development, mentoring and coaching, and strategic planning. He has been working in public education as a teacher, administrator, and professor for over twenty years.